GRATEFUL FOR THE
JOURNEY

GRATEFUL FOR THE
JOURNEY

SURVIVING COVID 19

TERRI BRINSTON

CITI OF BOOKS

CITIOFBOOKS, INC.
3736 Eubank NE Suite A1
Albuquerque, NM 87111-3579
www.citiofbooks.com
Hotline: 1 (877) 389-2759
Fax: 1 (505) 930-7244

Ordering Information:

Quantity sales. Special discounts are available on quantity purchases by corporations, associations, and others. For details, contact the publisher at the address above.

Printed in the United States of America.

ISBN-13:   Softcover   978-1-962366-18-2
              Hardcover   978-1-962366-19-9

Library of Congress Control Number: 2023917529

DEDICATION

To my mom, the woman who I admire most. You taught me how to love, fight, and stand up for myself. You taught me how to give and how to serve others. You taught me how to work hard and stay committed to whatever I do. Ultimately, you taught me how to be a powerful Black Woman, and for this, I thank you.

Love Terri

"If my people who are called by my name humble themselves, and pray and seek my face and turn from their wicked ways, then I will hear from heaven and will forgive their sin and heal their land." (2 Chronicles 7:14 ESV)

ABOUT THE AUTHOR

My name is Terri Brinston. Getting infected by COVID-19 was the hardest thing I had ever been through. I was raised in the Detroit Metropolitan Area and attended public school in Dearborn Heights, Michigan. I am a Christian. I cherish my family and friends. I have been happily married for over 29 years and blessed with two handsome boys. I hold a Master of Arts degree in Education Administration & Community Leadership from Central Michigan University and a Bachelor of Science in Nursing from Madonna University. I am a Registered Nurse and hold a Legal Nurse Consultant certification, too.

In addition to working as a pediatric nurse, I have more than two decades of experience teaching and consulting with schools, parents, and students. I'm the CEO of the Nurturing Wellness Group Foundation and My School Nurse. In my leisure time, I am actively involved in art and church ministries. I love serving others. Becoming infected with COVID-19 helped me redefine my purpose and solidified my commitment to my Christian faith. It is my prayer that my story does the same for you.

PREFACE

This book is based on the personal experiences that I encountered while being diagnosed and recovering from the horrible pandemic COVID-19. It focuses on the healing process, learning, gratitude, motivation, and spiritual energy that this journey has given me so far.

Until now, there have been more than five million cases of COVID-19 throughout the world. This horrible virus has killed entire families, devastated communities, and wrecked small businesses and major industries while leaving a trail of destruction and confusion as it disrupted our very way of life.

As my heart mourns for the victims who have suffered and continued to struggle during this horrific time, I am truly humbled and grateful that my life was spared and that I survived its wrath. God listened to my prayers and rewarded me for my uncountable trials. He turned my nightmare into a source of healing and rebirth and orchestrated an amazing symphony of events after that.

My work aims to focus on the spiritual side of my healing. I want to tell my readers how I continued to keep my faith in the Supreme Power while struggling to stay in this world. I know that many people who have lost their lives or are deeply impacted by this horrible virus could not cope with it as I did. There had been so much devastation and hardship for numerous people around the globe. Therefore, I can't thank the Lord enough for blessing me with a new life.

I want to inspire my readers to find hope and motivation to be their best selves, no matter what is happening around them. I wish that you find all the peace, happiness, and comfort that your heart has ever wished for. Just like me, someday your trials will end too, and you will be *'so very grateful for the journey.'* The only key is to trust the process and keep your faith solely in Him.

CONTENTS

chapter 1

INTRODUCTION

"Sometimes, the greatest storms bring out the greatest beauty...Life can be a storm, but your hope is a rainbow, and your friends and family are the gold."

—*Steve Maraboli*

Have you ever had a moment in your life when you wondered why you were alive? I'm pretty sure most, if not all, people have been in that position at least once in their lives. It is at a time when they sat by themselves, absorbing their surroundings. The people, the things, and the emotions – just how superficial it all felt. I remember sitting in my room in the new automatic recliner that my husband had abruptly purchased for my comfort after returning home from the hospital after 29 days. I was confused and disoriented by the additional space available to me – something about it felt a little odd.

The door to my bedroom was open. I could see straight down the hall where the additional bedrooms, a family room, and a kitchen awaited me. However, I was afraid that all of this was nothing but a dream. I kept asking myself whether I was finally home with my family. Was it the fact that I wanted to be reunited with them so badly that this felt like reality? It felt as though I was walking the fine line between the two. I could smell food cooking and heard dishes clinging as my husband prepared a meal for me. My heart felt full. I did not want to wake up only to learn that this was nothing but a mirage in the desert and that I was still confined in a small room back in the hospital where I had no choice but to lie in bed by myself, craving human touch. I did not want to wake up in a world where everyone was in a hurry to leave me as they put on their masks and struggled to move about in their constricted PPE (personal protective equipment). To save me from the disappointment of that realization, I was trying hard not to accept my reality because it felt unreal.

Slowly, I started to allow myself to get acquainted with this version of reality and let everything sink in. Finally, I had to make myself understand that the past 29 days were over, and I won the battle against the odds. At the same time, I could not help but think about all those people who lost their battles to this deadly virus called COVID-19. My mind was a storm of thoughts, but most of them circled around all the people whose lives were deeply impacted by this horrible pandemic. All I could think of were the countless stories of heartbreak, pain, trauma, and tragedy – all because of one deadly virus. Watching the news felt like walking into a nightmare with your eyes wide open because it was nothing but a loud reminder of all those who did not make it out alive.

Sitting safely in the comfort of my recliner – that is when I had my *moment* - I wondered why I was still alive. Thoughts about all those who were not here today were playing in my mind, as though they were my loop of hell. Why did they not make it? Why was I still alive? I was suffering from *Survivor's guilt*, as some may call it. That single question plunged me deeper into my thoughts and ultimately made me realize that my survival was nothing but a miracle.

All over the world, there have been over thirty million cases of COVID-19 (and counting), the disease caused by the coronavirus, and more than 2.03M deaths and counting (worldwide). This horrible virus has not only cost us a large number of human lives, but it has also devastated communities and wrecked small businesses and major industries alike. COVID-19 brought the whole world to a halt, leaving a trail of destruction everywhere it could reach. It altered our lives and changed the world we knew into an isolated one. It caused us to shut our doors and lock ourselves behind in the name of protection. It tore our lives apart.

There is no day that goes by when my heart does not mourn for the people who have suffered it and continue to fight their battle against it. Having been in their place, I know a lot about how painful and lonely it is. I am truly humbled and grateful that my life was spared, and I survived the wrath of this deadly virus. While I was infected with it, I started to keep an account of my experience as a way to process everything I was going through.

I was emotionally overwhelmed by the chaos I called my life. I needed to write down everything happening to me to save myself from falling into the pit of denial. When faced with hard times, our brains often convince us to go into denial by refusing to accept reality for what it is. I believe when we write our thoughts down, it gives them a new meaning. Consequently, we can understand them better in a different light. I know this because when I started to write about everything, I realized how seamlessly the events of my life were connected. It prepared me for the devastation that came shortly after being diagnosed with COVID-19 and throughout my healing journey.

It was only then that it became clear to me that God orchestrated an amazing symphony of events. He somehow guided my steps and turned a nightmare into a source of healing and rebirth. I am so *"Grateful for the Journey."* In fact, I got the inspiration for writing this book from this feeling of gratefulness. It took writing down my tangled thoughts on a piece of paper in the hopes of processing my grief for me. I realize how all the hardships I went through were intertwined. At that moment, I felt nothing but thankful for every single setback, every single misfortune, adversity, and trial in my life that God allowed me to go through.

Another major reason I am writing this book is that I am passionate about the future - our children. I firmly believe that while our school systems teach many valuable skills to the students, they do not address all the aspects necessary for them to succeed and thrive in life. It is this passion that makes me want to fill the gap existing between education and wellness.

I know it as well as the back of my hand because of the struggles I underwent as a student. I had a learning disability that resulted in a poor self-image and severely low self-esteem. Even though I had a strong support system at home, I still remember how I had a difficult time coping with my schoolwork while enduring bullying, shame, and emotional distress. The sad reality is that more often than not, while the school teaches you everything about the Pythagoras theorem, the history of the world, and even about what windmills are, they hardly ever teach children about how to deal with trauma or stress. Kids get to know about every single bone in the body but nothing about taking care of their emotional needs. Children are taught about how cancer can kill a person but not about the effect of ignoring their mental health and how that too can lead them to a dark path.

I believe that a significant cause of our students' challenges in school stems from the imbalance of their physical, emotional, and/or spiritual well-being. The causes of this imbalance are many, but some of the primary reasons are unstable home environment, unsupervised home, divorce, moving, abuse (drug, physical, and mental), foster care, mental illness, and medical conditions. I think these major areas, alongside minor ones, increase the stress that students must learn to cope with.

This lack of knowledge and skills to effectively deal with stress factors in their lives is one reason why a teen takes their life every hundred minutes. Suicide is the third-leading cause of death for young people between the ages of 15 and 24. The fact of the matter is that we all have certain expectations for life. We plan our futures and aim to shoot the stars. When faced with hardships, we find ourselves on the brink of losing our faith. Tragedy and hopelessness almost go hand in hand. When life keeps breaking through your door with one problem after another, hardly giving you the time even to breathe, the line between holding on to faith and letting go becomes quite thin. It's easier to question your existence's purpose in the grander scheme of things than fighting challenging situations.

At times like these, when you find yourself emotionally exhausted and tired of carrying all your burdens, you need something to hold on to - a little strand of faith. Growing up, children are taught to dream big. They are told that the sky is the limit. Schools encourage kids to chase their dreams, create their reality, and choose the profession they love and somehow subconsciously make them believe that nothing will ever hinder them from attaining that. So, when they step afoot in the real world and are slapped across their face by reality, they find themselves lost, demotivated, and confused. They find it hard to cope and fight the odds. Not every child has a supportive family.

Everything I have been through has made me sympathetic toward the challenges our students face today. I want to use my story and journey to tell people how important it is to equip our children with the tools to deal with stress and tragedy. When they are instilled with this belief that life is not perfect, things do not always go as you plan for them to, and regardless of how many times they get knocked down, as long as they are alive, their battle is not over.

I believe through sharing my story, I can help others find calm in their storm. I hope to help people realize that everything, every hardship, and every ease has a season. Sometimes, we get so lost in the chaos of the world that we forget there could ever be a greater purpose for our distress. We start to look down upon ourselves through a victimizing lens. The purpose of my book is to help raise awareness. It is to make people realize how it was crucial for me to go through the adversities I went through to reach a point of rebirth.

This entire book is based on my life. I will be sharing a lot of memories and events that happened before and after my exposure to COVID-19. I want to tell the readers through my personal story that sometimes it is essential for us to go through hard times. You know how they say that without pain, would we ever know joy? Without the bad times, would we ever appreciate the good? You see, life is not a television series where everything is always perfect. It is brutal, and bad things happen more often than we like them to. However, I want to tell you to always look for the light at the end of the tunnel because there is one.

Hopelessness will get you nowhere. Whenever you are stuck with misfortune, I want you to think about all the ways it could be good for you. As humans, we have limited knowledge, and we cannot possibly foresee the future. God knows what is better for us in every aspect of our lives. He shapes the events of our lives in such a way that they beautifully come together in the end, only for our betterment. Since we are shortsighted, we often fail to realize the bigger picture. The message of my book is merely the following. We must become more resilient individuals and teach our children the same values. Alongside teaching our kids everything about math, geography, or biology, we must teach them life's realities. Lastly, God uses tribulations as a way to strengthen us, so we must embrace them and move on in life with high hopes and full hearts.

chapter 2

THE FAMILY

"Family is not an important thing. It's everything."

—*Michael J. Fox*

As humans, we have a natural need to belong, and the first place this need gets fulfilled is through our family. While our initial family is the one, we are born into, we get to choose who we want to share our life with further on. My husband and I share two amazing boys. The thing about family is that it's always there. However, the term *family* implies different meanings for different people. Based on individual circumstances, a family can be small or large and close or distant. I am so grateful that I have a huge close family consisting of my immediate family, parents, siblings (four brothers and one sister), my husband's eight brothers and four sisters, a family of friends, and a church family.

Like most families, we are not without issues, but I know who I can count on when times get rough. When life gets hard and things look hopeless, my family lifts me up, and vice versa. We take care of each other when times are hard, we love each other through good and bad times, and we mean everything to one another. There is nothing you cannot do when you have your family on your side. At least, that's how my family makes me feel - *safe, understood, supported, and protected.* I am truly blessed to have them in my life. When I take a moment to think about it, I realize just how blessed I am to be married to someone as incredible as my husband. He is one of the most laid-back people I know. He has a *"Hakuna Matata"* type of personality, as I like to call it. On the other hand, I hate to admit it, I'm a little uptight and a little bougie, so I have been told. So we complement each other quite well. When you are a strong-headed person, you need a significant other who is quite the opposite, so they can help calm you down when needed. Over the years, I have needed him to calm me down often. I don't think there has ever been a time when my kids heard us argue or we went to bed angry. Whatever I am doing, no matter what the situation, he always supports me without question.

When we first got married, the place I was working at closed and relocated to Florida. We had just bought a house, so instead of relocating with the company, I ended up quitting. Since we had no kids at that point, we agreed that I would go to nursing school full time. While pursuing my degree, I became pregnant twice and was blessed with my two boys. I never skipped a beat. I took time off from school as needed with both pregnancies and immediately returned to the grind as soon as my doctor released me. My husband supported me all the way.

While pursuing my degree, I had the opportunity to go abroad and study mental health in England for four weeks. My kids are three years apart and the younger one was not even one year old at that time. Honestly, although my husband was great, he struggled with taking on parenting responsibilities at that time. Regardless of that, he stepped up and told me he would babysit the kids, and I should go to England. That's the thing I love the most about him. He always put me first and has always been my biggest supporter. Nevertheless, his parenting skills needed a little help. After his comment, "I will babysit the kids," yes, he actually said to *babysit* his kids. I honestly believed it would be good for my husband and the boys if I went away for a while. I thought he could bond with the boys and get a crash course in parenting without my interference. He would have an opportunity to experience fatherhood at its full intensity, i.e., without me being there to cook, clean, and dress the boys. I saw this as an opportunity, so I went to work and started scheming.

As mentioned before, my husband has a huge family, and I told them not to help out while I was gone; he would share with me when I called how odd it was that not one person offered to cook a meal or babysit. It's kind of funny when I think about it now because he never knew I went around telling my family not to help him, but it all worked out for the better in the end. Years later, when I graduated from nursing school, I told him it was his turn. I asked him what he wanted to do, whether he wanted to quit his job and take some time off or continue working. He told me he would love to take a break from working and decided to be a stay-at-home dad. I most definitely believe that his crash course in parenting guided his decision.

As my husband had always rooted for me in every aspect of my life, I agreed without a second thought. He formed an amazing bond with the boys because he was always around. He would pick them up from school, volunteer for school field trips, and even bake cookies when needed for their class. I was working as a pediatric nurse at that time, so I would work the midnight shift, and while I loved my family, I wasn't as involved in my kids' lives as my husband was. More often than not, I'd be sleeping when they came home from school.

However, one day, I decided to surprise my boys by going with my husband to pick them up. When we pulled up in the car to the gate, my husband got out, and I witnessed a grown woman, which happened to be my son's teacher, racing my son to my husband. I was as taken aback as any wife would be, and when he got back in the car, I looked at him and thought, 'Ok, oh, you need to take your ass back to work.' Not soon after that, we spoke about a plan for him to find a fulfilling opportunity. He found a great contingent job at a local community college as a clinical instructor. This was perfect for him.

Sometimes, I think back to all of it. It amazes me how much my partner sacrificed just to help me achieve my goals, how selflessly every time he allowed me to get what I needed. Whether it was working the night shifts or going to England when my youngest son was less than a year old, my husband never bailed out on me. Oh, by the way, my son didn't even know who I was when I returned from England because he was so young when I left.

There honestly are not many people in this world like my husband, someone who has never failed to fortify our kids or me. To this day, he continues to do so. This realization truly sunk in for me when I was about to be discharged from the hospital after 29 miserable days in isolation. They wanted to send me to a rehabilitation facility because I was still struggling with walking and needed a lot of care. The problem was that most of the rehabilitation centers were in nursing homes, and they did not want me. This recovery infected COVID-19 patients around their immune-compromised and high-risk residences. Although I felt pretty hopeless, to say the least, I understood. I decided to call my rock, my husband, and asked him whether he would be willing to take care of me if I came home. That man did not think twice and said he would. When I got back home, he would bathe me, apply lotion to my arms and back, comb my hair, and even braid my "kink-a-bugs," as he lovingly referred to my nappy hair. He took complete care of me. I became dependent on him, and when he was not in my presence, I became extremely nervous, and my anxiety would skyrocket.

It was a dark time for me because, having been isolated for a month before that, I had separation anxiety whenever my husband was out of my sight. I felt like he was not going to come back, and I would be left all alone. I was honestly a prisoner to my mind. My thoughts were like the chaos of a tornado. I kept struggling with drawing the line between reality and dreams. I had horrible night terrors, which led to hallucinations. I thought I was two people most of the time. I did not know if I was dreaming or if this was my new reality. Everything was a huge question mark to me. I hated that I could not organize my thoughts or reality. I mean, don't they say that the only person you can truly trust is yourself? How was I supposed to trust anything my mind told me when the line between reality and dreams was so blurry?

Being in the hospital by myself was a very scary and humbling experience for me. After I woke up from being on the ventilator, I thought I was in another country, deep in the Ciudad Perdida, the world's largest mega-slum in Mexico, and that I had been kidnapped. I was still in the ICU. No one looked familiar. My room was dark, dingy, and dirty. I smelled burning wood and saw particles flying around the room like ash. I heard Mexican dogs barking.

Don't ask me how I knew they were Mexican dogs. I was truly tripping but was terrified that the workers were going to torture me. I thought if I could just be good and polite, say please and thank you, and not bother those people in masks and gowns, they would not hurt me. I carried this fear with me even after I came back home. Even though I was physically there, mentally, I was in a parallel universe; one where nobody was allowed to be near me; where they wanted to be as far from me as they could.

When my husband went to the store, I would be extremely anxious because my mind kept telling me he would not come back, and I would have to return to Mexico. I was horrified by that possibility. Thank God my husband did not need to leave me too often. The blessing in all of this is the Lord knows I would need my husband home during this vulnerable time. My husband stayed home and nursed me back to health because he had taken my job a few months earlier.

I used to work at a public high school for over 20 years, and for a variety of reasons, they overlooked me for promotions for many years. I was finally offered an opportunity to step into a new role as the acting vocational director. I was meant to walk into this position that fall semester. My teaching schedule was abbreviated to fully devote two hours out of the day to my new role. To my surprise and disappointment, a week before school started, they told me that they had hired a consultant to do this job instead. I was devastated. It was straight unfair because number one, they had given me their word, and number two, I had worked hard over the years serving in many leadership roles and led numerous committees. You name it, and I had done it. On top of all of that, I was qualified with a master's degree in administration.

I was extremely disappointed but thought that 20 years was a long time just to walk away. When I got another job offer, I was hesitant at first because I had been loyal to them for so long, always participating in everything, getting nominated for teacher of the year, receiving grants, and making great partnerships for my program. I was a proven asset to the school, or that's what I thought, at least. I realized that I had been giving my all to that school for years, and they never gave me an opportunity.

Nevertheless, I did give this one a go. It so happened that I got a call from the principal of a different district offering me another job. I felt it was an excellent opportunity for me because the job description and pay were the same. It felt like a lateral move, and I could be effective at my new job because of my experience. Also, I was feeling very undervalued and mistreated.

Even nice people have their limits. The cherry on top of all of this was that they wanted me to accept the department head position instead of the position they promised me. This would have caused me to take the job away from a woman who had been doing it for over 18 years. I asked them whether she was doing a good job. They replied, "Yes, she is." I told them I did not understand why they would offer me her job when she was doing such a great job.. They responded that it would suit me better and that since they couldn't give me the job they promised me, they wanted to give me some sort of compensation. That was my last straw because everything aside, this was straight-up unethical.

I was frustrated to the core, so naturally, when that principal called me and offered a position to teach the same content that I was teaching, I took it as a sign from God. I knew that He opened the door for me. I just did not know why. After 20 years of being overlooked and mistreated, this time, I was ready to move on, and everything lined up perfectly.

I finally understood how I had been a victim of a lack of professional growth for so long. I was more than happy to leave, but I felt compelled to help them find my replacement. My first call was to my sister-in-law, Shanta, who had always wanted my amazing schedule. She was also an RN and I had just known she would jump to the opportunity to work from 7 a.m. to 2:30 p.m. Monday through Friday, no work on weekends or holidays, and three months off during the summer. She was working a 12-hour midnight shift from 7 p.m. to 7 a.m. every other weekend, on almost every holiday, and even all summer long. When I called her to tell her the great news, she refused. I was truly confused. Usually, I would have asked why and try to convince her that this was a great opportunity that does not come along often. When she said no, though, I just accepted it and was not persistent at all. She told me she was working in a different department and liked doing what she did. She liked being a nurse, and I told her I was happy for her. This was very odd for me, and although I was confused by my demeanor, I was at peace with her decision.

At this point, I told my husband to apply for my job. He was hesitant at first, saying that he thought it wasn't the best idea. I told him that I had already recommended him when I really had not at that time. I can be a little persistent at times. He applied for the job and got hired. This was the only reason he could be at home when I was at the hospital and take care of me when I came home.

Interestingly, the hospital I was admitted to while I had corona was the same one my sister-in-law, Shanta, was working at. In fact, she worked on the coronavirus floor. During this time, there were just a few patients admitted to her unit. I was admitted, and then a good friend of my brother was also admitted to the same floor. Then the floodgates opened, and the pandemic was in full effect. I don't need to tell you how the restrictions due to their contagiousness kept us isolated. People couldn't visit us, but because my sister-in-law was working there, she could be that connection to both our families, especially my husband, because she would come in, check on me, and provide a report for my husband.

When I think about it now, it's almost like it was all planned out that way, you know? I mean, if only one thing had changed and happened differently, a lot of others would be affected consequently. For instance, if I had not have been fed up with my job, I would not have left. If my sister-in-law had taken my job, it would have been harder for my husband to manipulate his schedule to care for me when I was discharged from the hospital. It was a job she had wanted for as long as I can remember, and when the time came, she turned it down. The fact that it all worked out so well is what amazes me. That's what I mean by us not understanding God's reasoning behind events in our lives. I could have convinced my sister-in-law to take the job. I can be very convincing, as I mentioned. I could have talked her into it, but I didn't. I let it go, and it unfolded like this. The next time you're in a tough position, remember it is part of a grander scheme. Remember that life is not what you see over the surface. Things go much deeper than they initially look.

"If you think their messy room is hard to look at, just wait till it's empty."
- Unknown

The bond a mother shares with her son is an unbreakable one. As said before, I have two sons. My older son's name is Travis, and since he is the firstborn, I share a special bond with him. This was also because I was always around for the first few years of his life more than I was for my second son. I would go to the market and buy local fresh-grown produce, bring it home, carefully wash it, cut it up and puree it, and make all his baby food. I was extremely particular about what he wore, the detergent I used, who he was around, and who touched him – you know, the usual first-time mom precautions. It was an entirely new and exciting experience for me. I loved him with all my heart. It was a love that I had never experienced before. When I brought him home, I remember praying and asking God to help me raise him to be a strong, loving, and God-fearing husband and father. I did not care how tired or exhausted I was and how much I had on my plate, I would always make him my priority. Being a mother would genuinely make me feel like a superwoman at times.

If you're a parent, you know how that phrase *"time flies"* really fits in well when it comes to children growing up. One minute you see them take their first steps and say their first words, and the next thing you know is they are all grown up, leaving for college. I feel it was just yesterday; my son would get excited seeing balloons and how with perfect aim, he would pop people in the face leaving them stunned by the amount of strength this little guy had.

I still remember how devastated I was when my husband and I drove Travis to college. He was leaving home for five years to become an electrical engineer. Although it was just about a 45-minute-long drive, I cried the entire way back, and my husband said it was the longest ride he had ever been on. I was especially close to Travis, and when he left us, even though it was just for college, I felt like I was dying. I was extremely heartbroken. There is nothing in the world that can fill that space of your child. I did not care how old he got. To me, he was always my baby boy.

Once he graduated, he moved to Oklahoma to work. That pushed him further away from me. I was heartbroken all over again because I thought that he'd come back home post-graduation. The anxiety of him being so far away was too much for me to bear. He wasn't just 45 minutes away now. He might as well have been on the other side of the world. He's always been a loving young man, so he saw how anxious I was getting, and to help put me at ease, he installed a tracker on his phone for me to always know where he was. He wanted to make sure I had access to his location at all times, so every time I felt anxious, I could just check where he was, and I would feel better. It was an amazing gesture because I know that kids often feel relieved when they are out of their parent's sight, knowing they have the freedom to do whatever they want. He cared more about my feelings than his privacy.

While at a bachelor party in Kentucky, Travis went to a lake with his friends and dislocated his shoulder from the water's surface tension when he dove into the water. His friends had to jump in the water to pull him out and rushed him to the hospital. When I got a phone call telling me my baby was hurt, I felt like the ground slipped from beneath my feet. He ended up needing surgery, so when he got back to Oklahoma, I got on the first flight I could catch to Oklahoma and flew there to be with him and take care of him. After his surgery, I brought him back home so I could take better care of him. It was an excellent opportunity for us to bond because it had been a while since we spent quality time together. I got the chance to develop an adult relationship with him and know him as a man. Since I was nursing him back to optimal health, we spent a lot of time together, and I am grateful for it. It was like we were catching up on all those years he had been away from home. I was getting to know this new version of him and loved every bit of it. I was extremely impressed and felt proud, realizing my husband and I did a great job raising Travis.

When I was admitted to the hospital with COVID, Travis and my husband had an opportunity to rekindle and strengthen their bond. Since they could not visit me in the hospital, they relied on one another and shared the responsibility of calling the hospital and getting updates on my status while I was on the vent in the ICU.

I love being a mother. I even enjoyed being pregnant. You could not tell me I was not pretty. I felt beautiful during both of my pregnancies, but my pictures revealed a much different reality. Thank God we did not have cell phones for selfies, and I had to wait to develop the film. I felt even more beautiful when I was pregnant with my youngest son Terrance. I was calm and extremely patient while carrying him. I would need this new disposition with my pretty boy. With Travis, though, I was mean and extremely agitated about everything. My husband would try and redirect my wrath away from him and onto other people.

I remember this one day; I was angry for no particular reason. He was volunteering as a little ledge baseball coach, and the city would not open the bathrooms for students to use during practice. He asked me to call the director and fight his case. I called the director and unleashed my rage on him. Oh my, I feel kind of bad thinking about it, but the next day he brought my husband the key to the bathroom because one of his parents ripped him a new "ass whole," he said.

As I said, I was totally the opposite in the case of Terrance. During my pregnancies, it was like I took on the character that was specifically needed for each child. Travis was mild-mannered, so I was aggressive and acted as his protector. Terrance, on the other hand, was self-reliant and independent, so I was laid-back and reserved.

While carrying Terrance, I was in nursing school during the entire pregnancy. I remember taking exams while having my face planted over a garbage can, trying to get my second wind between barfing. I was on my home stretch of completing school, so my husband picked up a lot of the slack. Terrance was pretty independent. He always wanted to keep up with his older brother. So, he would do whatever he could to keep up with him. He was always in some type of competition. In fact, by the time he was four years old, he could ride his bike without the training wheels.

Anyone with more than one child knows that the second child wants to grow up too fast. They want to be able to do everything their elder sibling does, sometimes even better than him, all under the tab of competitiveness. He has quite a combative personality sometimes and has always been stubborn and hard-headed, which I'm positive he gets from his father. At the same time, Terrance has a nurturing spirit and has always been quite a passionate child. He works hard for what he wants, and I'll take the credit for that one. When it was time for him to go to college, he chose to study pre-med at the University of Toledo, which his cousins and brother Travis also attended. At that point, it was his desire, and frankly speaking, his grades showed it. He did well.

My sons grew up being extremely close to their cousins. They did everything together, and we even took them on vacation with us. It was totally for selfish reasons. They stayed out of our hair, and because they got distracted by their cousins, they were deterred from fighting or bickering with each other. This allowed us to enjoy our vacations truly. While attending college after finals, my boys, alongside their cousin William, went to a house party off-campus. While there's nothing out of the ordinary about three college students hanging out and celebrating the end of a semester, what happened caused them all to develop deep emotional scars. While they arrived at the party and my sons went into the house directly, my nephew went back to his car to get something. When he was out there, some boys held him at gunpoint, pulled him down an alley, and robbed him. As if that was not enough, they even hit him with the gun's back and broke his jaw. With the little strength he had left, he managed to get up and make it to the house where the party was ongoing, and everyone was oblivious to what had just happened. When they saw him, everyone came out, and he was immediately taken to the hospital.

On the other side, my younger son got in his car and drove back to our house in Michigan. My husband and I were sitting on the patio when he came and asked us if we had any idea what was happening. I had never seen him so terrified. All the color had drained from his face. His eyes were full of horror. All he could say was, "If we had walked out of the house, we would all be dead." We were in shock by this extremely disturbing news. William is like a son to us, and we were devastated. As parents, we raise our children to be kind and responsible citizens. We work hard, pouring everything we can into them to prepare them for this cruel world and afford them proper education and a fulfilling future.

Nonetheless, we have no control over the road they may travel. Quite frankly, the only thing we can do is pray - pray for a hedge of protection around them. I know that our prayers were answered that night. Our boys were spared, and God provided that hedge of protection.

Although William was severely injured, he survived. I am so grateful he did. The boys were quite traumatized by this event, and I regret that we did not have our boys seek counseling support. I think this event played a major role in my son falling into a dark depression. This was the beginning of Terrance's downfall. Everything in his life went downhill from there. He started to spiral, got into some unhealthy relationships, and even explored drugs a little more than a typical college kid. The truth is that we all have different ways to process our trauma. Some people go to therapy, some do drugs, some get addicted to antidepressants, and the list goes on. When you almost get acquainted with death, you start viewing your life from a different perspective. Some people drown in the sorrows of those "have-been/could-have-been" things. Because he was not living at home, I had no idea that he had been doing drugs to the point where he was almost always under some influence. The thing about drugs is that they temporarily fade all your pain and make you feel like you're on top of the world and even out of it. When they die down, reality and its ugliness hit you like a bullet at full speed, and you want to run away from confronting it, so you keep consuming drugs and alcohol just so that you never have to accept hard truths or face your fears. That's why people do things they are afraid of when they're high because the fear aspect fades away. Another thing is that, like every other thing, your body starts to develop tolerance to your usual dose, so you just have to keep increasing it for it to hit you or make you high.

It's the same with everything - medicines, caffeine, anything that is supposed to affect your body – too much of it leads to tolerance. This is why he kept experimenting with harder and harder things. His life was rapidly going downhill. He started performing very badly at college, to the point where he had to drop out and come home. He began to get his life back on track with our help and went to truck driving school. I believe a parent's job is never done. When our kids are young, they have our time and patience. When they are older, they have our hearts and mind. We cannot give up on our children. In God's word, He shares a parable of the Prodigal Son - a son receives his inheritance and travels to a distant country, wastes all his money in wild extravagance, becomes desperately poor, returns to his father, and is still received with open arms. Prodigal, here and elsewhere, means rashly or wastefully extravagant. Although my son did not have any inheritance to waste, he did have shit loads of opportunities and talents. Terrance started working as a truck driver after that and moved out. He was doing well, but his depression and anxiety became overwhelming. We all thought that he was only smoking marijuana. How bad could it be, right? The reality was that he had started to fall deep into depression to the point where he had to come back home, but this time, he had a new addition to his family, his dog Zeus.

My husband has never been a fan of dogs, and he refused to keep Zeus, saying that our house was not dog friendly. I told him that I loved my son more than the house, so if he were depressed, we would get him a whole support system, not shut him out. However, he was entirely against it. Firm to his decision, he insisted that we should take Zeus to the Human Society, so someone else could adopt him.

The Human Society posted an ad for Zeus so the community could see he was available for adoption. He looked pitiful in the ad. Most people started commenting to shame the person who had put the advert up, saying who would be heartless enough to put a dog for adoption or get rid of it? When Terrance saw those comments, he was devastated and genuinely upset. I called a friend of mine, a psychologist, and asked her how I should tackle the situation. She told us that we needed to get the dog back, and so we did. It was very difficult having a dog in our home.

It required a lot of work trying to keep the house clean and tidy. Although Terrance did look after him very well, having a dog impacted the cleanliness of my home. Sometimes, I just had to stop and count to ten to hold it together. Although we struggled with the transition of having Terrance and Zeus home, God had a way of making lemon into lemonade. The truth is that when I was hospitalized, Zeus and Terrance together were great support for my husband. Zeus was exactly the comfort my husband needed. Terrance went to work, and since my older son was in Oklahoma, my husband would be home alone. When he was sad or crying, Zeus would come and lie his head on his knee or lie at his feet when nobody was home. He became a great companion for my husband - someone who he did not have to justify his sadness with.

Exactly two weeks before I was admitted to the hospital, my husband and I were at a conference, and we got a phone call out of the blue. Terrance was on the phone, and I could hear him yelling, asking if it was me, he was speaking to. I replied in the affirmative, and he was like, "No, this is not my mom! Put my mom on the phone!" I was taken aback and confused. I asked him what was going on and whether he was okay. He was with a friend who told us that he had taken acid and was having a terrible trip. He was combative and irrational.

His friend even told us that she had no idea he had consumed it. I remember how my heart was racing. I was worried out of my mind. I had no idea what to do because I was at the conference without a car, and they were up north, just far enough for me not to be able to get to him. I told his friend to call an ambulance immediately, and she hung up, saying she would do that. As a mother, knowing her son is in such a wrong place, I hated feeling helpless, and all I could do was pray at that point. After a short while, his friend called me, informing me that the police were also called because it was a drug issue. I was much more scared of the fact that the police were coming than I was of this lousy trip because I feared they would not be patient with him. My son was not a little guy, and his state of mind might have added to his stocky frame. I truly feared for his life. I did not want them to shoot him. When you are in the middle of such a situation, you naturally always assume the absolute worst outcome of everything.

I told his friend that she had to calm him down some way before the police came. My heart was heavy and filled with fear. I did not want to imagine what the police were going to do when they arrived. I started to pray. At that point, my husband and I knew nothing we could do except pray for him. I hung up the phone when the police arrived. I was afraid and clearly understood and related to the "Black Lives Matter" movement. Police brutality is a real fear for us, i.e., those raising black men. I know it is hard for some to believe, but it is real. I was paralyzed with fear.

Sometime later, we got another call from one of Terrance's friends. She told us that the police did not get into the house. They allowed the paramedics to handle the situation. God is so good. Terrance managed to calm down and allowed them to help him. When we returned home, we talked to him about the incident. He told us that he felt like he was living in a loop of his personal hell during his trip - one where he had no choice but to relive every bad decision he had ever made over and over again. He said he could not get out, and he had started to hallucinate and have an awful experience.

Over the next few days, he was terrified. He had PTSD from those hallucinations because he kept remembering the episodes playing in his head and reliving the trauma repeatedly. He was afraid to do anything because he did not want to face his fears again or relive that traumatizing experience. I had never seen him like that in my life. He went from this bright, ambitious child to someone terrified of sleeping.

As a mother, it broke my heart into a million pieces. I knew that I had to get him some help, and so I did. He soon stopped doing drugs and started to recover slowly but surely. Once he was clean, things started to look better for him, and his life started to fall into place.

When I was finally diagnosed with COVID and hospitalized, I realized now that I am so happy all of that happened to my son. It might sound like a harsh thing to say, but we don't realize that sometimes we have to go through pain and trauma to change our lives, clear our lens, and grow from it. I always prayed to God to make him miserable in his sin, not because I wanted my baby to go through pain, but because I wanted him to understand the impact of his choices. Weed is the first step. It's a gateway to more potent drugs, and everyone knows that. Through his misery and terrible trip, he learned that he had to leave drugs behind and change his whole life.

I think about how if all of this had not happened, and he had been under the influence when I went to the hospital, it would have been even more of a traumatic experience for my family. Moreover, I often think about whether he would even have been able to survive the news of me being hospitalized because he would have just taken more drugs to cope with it all. After all, that was just how he dealt with life. Anything even a little unsettling happened, and he would smoke until it stopped mattering or affecting him. Thus, I am genuinely grateful that when he got off the drugs, he started to develop a stronger relationship with Christ, connecting with our pastors and talking to different family and close friends. He was not ashamed. He would talk about what he was going through very easily and be quite upfront and transparent. When I was in the hospital, instead of doing drugs to relieve his pain, he cried and allowed himself to feel emotions.

The thing I think about often is that when I was in the hospital, I was not worried about them. Usually, even when I would have to go out of town for something, I would worry about my younger son a lot because of everything he had endured. However, when I was hospitalized, I was not worried about my sons or even my husband. I was at peace because I knew they had each other despite the odds and were close to one another. We had built an amazing network of friends and family, and I knew they would step in as needed. I had nothing to worry about. I could just focus on what I was going through without the burden of worrying about my family. God had them.

That's just the thing about life and circumstances, you know? All these instances and everything that happened was the Lord's way of using the situation to give everyone the support they needed – to help bring my family back together so that they could go through this pain together. We do not realize the importance of things when they happen because we feel stuck and suffocated at the time, but only when it's over, we understand how it was exactly what we needed.

chapter 3

THE BUSINESS

"Every great dream begins with a dreamer. Always remember, you have within you the strength, the patience, and the passion to reach for the stars to change the world."

—*Harriet Tubman*

Mostly, the things we do best in life are those we are deeply passionate about. The undying flame of passion for what we do emerges from a heartfelt story of a far-away time – one we never seem to forget, one whose shadow we can never outrun. No matter where we go in life, it sticks with us like a tattoo. The best part about being a Christian is that if we believe and trust God, He will tip the scales in our favor, use that story to do something great, and give our experiences a profound purpose.

My flame sparked when I was a little girl. I was in elementary school when they identified me as a special-ed student. That was the first time I recognized that I was different, but not the good kind of difference where the teachers tell your parents that you're gifted and should be studying with smarter individuals. It was quite the opposite, actually - the kind that makes you feel like you're the ugly duckling in the pond, the one that doesn't belong. It set the stage for extremely low self-esteem and a highly self-conscious personality for me.

I was very delayed, so I could not read or spell. As a little girl, watching every other child around me do everything I struggled to do with ease really crushed my spirits. I started believing that I was dumb and ugly and that it was somehow my fault that I was not good enough like the others. I felt as though I was a loser and as if attending special-ed classes were not embarrassing enough for me. The other kids would also tease me and make fun of the fact that I was different.

Why me? The mind of a child.

Terri Brinston

"Why do I have to be so consumed with fear, anxiety, frustration, and shame? Why do I have to feel so insignificant and alone? I'm a good person. I love people, well, most people. I love life. I come from a good family. My parents love me. I have a great home with everything I could ever want. I'm healthy. People even say I'm quite attractive. So why me? Did I do something wrong? Is God mad at me? Am I cursed to be stuck in this emotional wreck of a life? I hate to go to school. I am sick with worry each and every day. I know my mom thinks I'm crazy. Each day I get up and beg my mom to let me stay home. I get myself so worked up that I even believe that I am physically sick. My head, heart, my stomach hurt, I have bad cramps. I would make up whatever excuses I could to convince mom to let me stay home. I do not want to face another day of shame and utter torment. I am too ashamed to tell my own mom. She knows I struggle, but she does not have any idea how much I struggle emotionally. She is so proud of me and has so much on her hands that I don't want to add to it. Who can I tell, who can I talk to?

Another day back at school, my pleading did not work. Back to this learning institution, a hurdle that I must jump before I am free. Freedom - I dream of it often. Freedom to me is a day without tears or a lump in my throat that develops when I try to hold them back. Freedom is having peace of mind, wholeness, confidence, and pride. I only yearn for a day, one day! I know I don't deserve more than that. I see freedom in CeCe each day. CeCe is the nickname I call my big sister Semon. I wish I had what she has. Glowing with confidence and speaking with authority, she is a beautiful black woman with style and pride. She has no restrictions and comes in or goes out as she pleases. I wish she would teach me how to be like that. I'm just a kid to her with a decade gap between us. She doesn't even know how much I admire her as she is too busy with her crazy friends. I hate her friends with passion. I treat everyone nicely but them. She doesn't understand why I treat them so meanly and she never will. They had all her attention and left me with none.

I sit in class; dreading being called on to read. My hands are sweating, and my heart is pounding out of my chest. I feel like I'm just going to fall out of my desk. I can't catch my breath and want to scream. Please don't call on me! Can anyone see me or feel my pain? The agony that I am going through - can anyone help me? Please help me. Everyone will laugh at me; I know it. They will talk about me; I just know it. I find myself counting paragraphs and trying to pre-read my passage before it is my turn to read. If only I could practice sounding out the words before my turn and get control of my emotions long enough to focus. I can't. I can't do it. I must get out of this class. I must go now. My hand shoots up almost unconsciously, and with a sincere plea, I ask, "May I go to the restroom? I am not feeling well. Here come the stares. The cold eyes of judgmental teenagers and the whispers, "She's always sick."

Well, I escaped that horrible ordeal - now on to the next one of trying to escape anyone seeing me going to my special class. Why is it at the entrance of the busiest hallway of the school? Obviously, these people have no idea how their decision to assign this class to this room would have such a dramatic effect on me. Who do I need to talk to? Who can I tell? Who am I kidding? Who would listen to me? So, I had to take matters into my own hands and waste time in the locker room until the halls were just about empty, and I could dart into the room before anyone saw me.

I don't have any real friends - no one who I could truly trust with my secret or one who would truly relate to my struggle. NO ONE!! Sure, I have girls and boys who I like to be around from time to time, but I don't trust anyone. I am guarded and on alert. I would not even want to be my friend. I am ashamed, embarrassed, and outright paranoid. People say I'm quiet and shy. They don't know me. I'm not shy. I am bursting with passion, desire, and ambition. I'm very absorbent. When you don't talk, you have a lot of time to watch people and observe their behavior and interaction. I guess you could say that I'm a people watcher, a spectator. A spectator is someone who watches and looks at but is not involved or experiencing - someone who watches life happen. I daydream a lot. This helps distract me, so I'm not so consumed with my situation. That is my secret."

> # LORD
> Enlighten what's dark in me,
> Strengthen what's weak in me,
> Mend what's broken in me,
> Bind what's bruised in me,
> Heal what's sick in me,
> And lastly,
> Revive whatever peace and love
> has died in me.
> Amen.

As I think about my early years, I can't help but shed a tear just thinking about how I suffered in silence. It truly saddens me even today, but time has given me wisdom, and I know that I would not be who I am today without the struggles of yesterday. My secret, as I so innocently called it, is the foundation of my story.

Whenever I think back to my childhood, the one thing I most strongly recall is how much shame I carried with me. When you're a kid, life is supposed to be simple. However, due to my learning disability, I always felt like an outsider – someone who did not fit in. I was so embarrassed and ashamed of myself that growing up, I hardly made any friends. I never wanted to give someone the chance to see me up close because that would mean they would find out my secret. I did not think I was different but just straight-up stupid and incompetent. Nevertheless, my mom was my best friend. She was the one who comforted me when I was lonely and gave me hope when I was hopeless. She was and continues to be my biggest cheerleader. Due to her tireless support, I always knew that I was going to be okay. I did not know how, but my mom believed in me much more than I believed in myself.

In high school, kids who have learning disabilities are put through a career preparation program or vocational school to give them a chance at making a living for themselves without having to go through college. Since I fit the description of children with impaired learning abilities, I completed a cosmetology program during my senior year of high school. When I graduated, I received my cosmetology license, which meant I could do hair and pursue that as my career. That was my reality, and I accepted my fate. God had another plan for me. Sometimes, He uses extremely difficult situations to redirect your path.

My dad was diagnosed with cancer a few years after I graduated from high school. This was devastating for my entire family. He was a hardworking provider, a firm, an army veteran, and a real class act. I loved to watch him shave with his shaving cream and a razor, and the way the house smelled when he smoked his pipe and an occasional cigar. He was a gentleman. Not only did I love my dad dearly, but I also respected him. He spent his last days at home, although he was placed in hospice. I remember one day, as I was caring for him, he looked at me with hopeful eyes and told me I should be a nurse. I was genuinely taken aback. Firstly, I thought he forgot who he was talking to for a second. I was a kid who struggled with studies all my life. How could I be a nurse? It almost sounded like a joke. He was persistent with his recommendation, and the seed was planted. That was the first time I actually thought that I could look at another opportunity for myself.

From where I stood, it felt impossible for me to even think of being a nurse. Nurses are smart and respected – the total opposite of who I thought I was. Nevertheless, my father told me he believed in me, and there is nobody I respect more than my parents. Knowing that he thought this was something I could do planted a seed of hope in me. I think sometimes we just need someone to believe in us despite the odds. Someone to tell us that regardless of what the world says, we are destined for great things.

After battling cancer for as long as he could, my father passed away. However, he gave me the greatest gift before he left. His belief in me gave me hope. That was all I needed to explore the possibility of becoming a nurse. I ended up getting help with my reading and focused entirely on my education. I will not say that college was easy because it was not, but I believed in myself and wanted to be everything my mom and dad thought I could be. Especially since he had passed away, I committed myself fully to achieving this goal. God also gave me my husband, so I was surrounded by family to keep me moving forward. I knew that if my dad thought I had what it takes to be a nurse, I was definitely cut to be one. Sure, I struggled a lot along the way. I took every English class, reached out whenever I needed help, and told myself that quitting was not an option. I was an older student compared to others and even had my children during college, but that never stopped me for a second.

All that hard work eventually paid off, and I did end up becoming a registered nurse. I was proud of myself and knew that my father would have been proud of me too. After graduating, I started working as a pediatric nurse in a hospital. In all honesty, I enjoyed working with children. Alongside that, I was working in the youth department at my church, basically teaching Sunday school. I developed a great passion for learning and teaching, which was quite odd, considering all that I had gone through. God had a plan despite everything.

A year or so after I started working as an RN, my neighbor graduated from college with a teacher's certificate, so she threw a party at her house to celebrate. When I got to the party, I met the principal of the school, where she had accepted a teaching position. Coincidentally, he happened to mention that there was a position available for a Health Occupations Instructor and to apply for it, you had to be an RN. Among other things, I was shocked that this opportunity fell right into my lap. I mean, I had been working as a nurse, and frankly, I did not love it because I was on a **Med-Surg/Pediatrics unit** that provides care for a wide range of medical conditions. The unit I worked on supported children with all types of disorders. It did not matter whether the pediatric patients had lead poisoning or cancer. They all came in the same unit. In a nutshell, I was stressed out every day. I would pray the entire way to work, from the parking deck to my unit, "Lord, please don't let me kill anyone today!"

At the party, I went up to the principal and started talking to him. He told me that there was someone else the current teacher had recruited for the position, but I should apply. I thought it was worth a shot since I had developed a passion for teaching. If I didn't get it, I still had my old job. So, I did not see any harm in applying. Luckily, I ended up getting the job. But was it really luck? I was overjoyed because I knew this opportunity would help me make a difference in these students' lives.

Growing up with such a profound reading disability, I never wanted any kid to undergo what I went through. Sometimes, the hardships we go through in life are meant to make us empathetic and kind. I taught and introduced my students to the medical field simultaneously by teaching them basic skills they could use in the medical field. It was like the best of both worlds. I ended up recognizing that there were students who struggled as I did back in school, and knowing how much it affected me, I knew I had to do something.

Only when I started believing in myself, I could let go of all the pent-up negative beliefs. So, I knew that if these kids were ever to reach great heights, they needed to believe in themselves. I had to teach them to dismiss their self-limiting beliefs and ignore those voices in their heads that told them they were not good enough. Therefore, I developed a program within my classroom in which I dealt with this particular area before I taught them anything.

I made them understand that nobody is perfect, everyone has shortcomings, but none of it defines them as a person; because if it did, I would not be where I am in life. I would tell them stories of my shortcomings and experiences to resonate with them and work harder. I did everything in my capacity to make them believe in themselves because, at the end of the day, the first step to achieving anything in life is believing in yourself. I knew that if I could help change the way they thought, I could help change their future. The best part of it all was that it worked. They were transparent with me and never hesitated to ask for help. They knew that I understood what they were going through, and I would never judge them.

Soon, I realized that it was not just my students who were having this issue. There were more kids, and I knew that I had to do something more to reach them. That is one of the reasons that I started my company, My School Nurse, to educate teachers on how to work with students who have medical issues. The fact of the matter is that having learning disabilities is not the only thing that affects a child's self-esteem or academics.

I teach teachers how to work with kids who struggle with a medical condition, for instance, if they have a chronic disorder like diabetes, asthma, or any other medical issue that impacts that child's ability. I also realized that many children were struggling with mental health issues because of losing family members or having a dysfunctional environment at home. I taught the teachers how to care for them in the classroom the right way because many schools do not have nurses. Thus, the students' best bet was for their teachers to understand what they were going through. I knew that sometimes we all just want to feel understood, and through educating the teachers, I could help their students feel safe and understood. Like they were not outcasts for being different or going through problems because it was normal. We all go through something. Everyone has their baggage and barriers that may prevent us from being successful and truly walking out our purpose.

When I went that route with business, My School Nurse, I saw that the program I had put together to help my students was powerful because they had started to bloom. Therefore, I added a program called "Life Support for Students" to my business. The program was designed to empower young people who have barriers that keep them from becoming successful. The whole concept was to help kids let go of their negative self-beliefs and start believing in themselves. They are transformed.

The interesting part is that it all started in my classroom. I used to teach cognitive behavioral therapy with my program and help my students overcome their self-doubts through it. When I realized how much it was benefiting my students, I extended it to young adults too. One major reason for this was that my own children were young adults at that point, and I thought if I could not help the people who were close to me, how could I say I trusted my own process? So, I put my boys and my nephews through it too. I did an online pilot through a Zoom session with the young adults in my family and, in no time, I realized how beneficial it was. The results were fruitful, as always. Thus, I figured if it were good for my kids, it would be good for others too.

Since I knew that funding youth-based programs was not easy, I started a non-profit organization. I made that curriculum a part of it, calling my non-profit "The Nurturing Wellness Group Foundation." The curriculum taught the concepts that helped me overcome my learning disability and the trauma of COVID-19. My program consists of seven models that are somehow bound together with four specific belief themes threaded throughout it to help govern a person's thoughts and decisions. The idea is that if you maintain these four themes, it will secure your ability to stay true to your commitments and obtain extraordinary heights.

"Our deeds determine us, as much as we determine our deeds."

-George Eliot

The first belief theme is *integrity*. People often take the power of integrity for granted. **Integrity** means following your moral or ethical convictions and doing the right thing in all circumstances, even if no one is watching you. Having **integrity** means you **are** true to yourself and would do nothing that demeans or dishonors you.

To be successful, you have to be true to who you are and honor your word. Never be ashamed of yourself. You're not different. You're unique and special in a good way. Use your integrity as a superpower.

The second belief theme is *strengthening your network*. We often fail to realize the value of the people around us. If you want a shot at being successful, it requires building a network of healthy and transparent relationships. It helps us at different stages in life, whether it's a time when we need a shoulder to cry on or someone to help us through a problem. I remember when I started to get COVID symptoms, the first person I thought about calling was Paul, one of my business associates, who is also a paramedic. He was the one who told me to go to the hospital. My sister-in-law Robin is a nurse practitioner. Her husband Mike, who is a doctor, helped me make the difficult decision to go on the Ventilator Throughout my stay, my other sister-in-law Shanta was my family's lifeline because she worked in the same unit I was admitted to. Moreover, when I started to lose hair, I connected to people I knew from my cosmetology program. I could go on and on naming how many family members and friends played a part in my recovery - people who prayed, picked up groceries, cooked a meal, cleaned my house, sent money, cards, and text messages, called, and just showered love on us during this extremely difficult time. It was amazing. I have never felt so loved.

The fact of the matter is that establishing and maintaining relationships with people is important. It's what got me through this entire time. Whether I needed medical assistance or was having mental health problems, I knew someone in every field. The reason for that is that I take my relationships seriously, as you should. When all is said and done, it's the people in your life who tend to you. When you're stuck with a calamity, they're the ones who become your rock to fall back on, so don't take them for granted.

The third concept is *being in action*. It's about taking control of your life, doing things you talk about doing, and bringing life to the phrase *"put your money where your mouth is."* Successful people don't just talk big. They prove everything they talk about through their actions.

The fourth and last concept is being *charitable*. Giving to charity does not always mean taking a good amount of money and giving it off to some nonprofit organization. Being charitable also means that you're willing to help people, doing things for someone other than yourself. Utilizing your time, talents, and treasures to bless others. Success is not limited to your personal and financial goals. It's also about the kind of person you are.

You know how they say, *"A little kindness goes a long way."* Life is really about the little things. During the time I was hospitalized, there was a point where I had been on the ventilator for three weeks. My body was slowly reaching a point where my organs were at risk of shutting down. Robin, my sister-in-law, called my husband and told him that I had been on the vent much too long and they had to do something. She told him they had to make a miracle happen or they would lose me. She started a prayer line in my honor. They got permission to put a phone near me while I was in the ICU.

While I lay there unconscious, with a machine breathing for me, they turned the phone toward me so I could hear the prayers. As people began to find out, they started joining the call. Soon, there were over a hundred people on the line who were just praying for me. Not only the people I knew, but there were literal strangers - people from different faiths, cultures, walks of life, and even different states. All of them came together just to pray for my recovery. My husband told me when they were praying, he could hear the machines going crazy, beeping, buzzing, and dinging. The nurse assured them that my vitals were fine and that I was reacting to their prayers.

Within four days of these prayers, I was brought off the ventilator. I was taken aback when my husband told me about this because I still remember how I grew up thinking I was not important, and yet, so many people, along with strangers, cared about my health and prayed for me. If anything, it was the most humbling experience ever.

Once I recovered, I asked Robin to continue the prayer line because while I may be well, there are always countless people who are hurting. Robin is beautiful inside and out. Her selflessness and impeccable commitment to her friends and family are unreal. I am so blessed to have her in my life.

Moving forward, I made it a point to be a part of this prayer line because if a stranger in some part of the world helped me through it, I'd love to be a stranger to another person. I listen to the prayer line every Monday and have had the chance to talk to some participants' families on the other end. When I tell them about my experiences, sometimes they're awestruck too, not by me but by how God works amazingly.

It's times like these that really put a lot of things in perspective for you. I realized how I have come such a long way, how much I have grown over the years, and how hard it was for me to let go of my self-defeating beliefs and let people in. I had to push myself to change my life because these self-limiting beliefs we grow up with often become strongholds in our lives. Even years down the lane, we wear a huge "self-doubt" chip on our shoulders and live life second-guessing everything we do.

Currently, we are working with foster care children and young adults who are aging out of foster care. We help them straighten the course of their lives and redirect their future. This is an issue that is dear to my partner and program director, Carla. She brings passion to this initiative due to her connection to this issue. One of the many things we share with this group is that they are the authors of their lives. We give them the tools to be able to reclaim their destiny because coming from broken families can have a profound impact on kids. They need someone to believe in them, and I'm glad my team and I can play that part. Carla's leadership in this initiative is priceless and further confirms my point that the Lord has a purpose for our pain.

Sometimes, I think that one of the reasons I experienced so much was to be able to use my experiences to give other people hope. I help them live vicariously through every incident I share with them to help them grow and become better versions of themselves. I know for a fact that if I had not gone through every test, I would not have a testimony. If I had not faced these trials and gotten through them, I would never have been able to have such a great impact. When you can resonate with someone else's pain, they tend to listen to you more, too, because they know you're not just throwing comforting words around like confetti. They know that you've been there, done, and felt that, too. Thus, when you tell them that it will be okay, they believe you, not because you sound reassuring, but because you got burnt by the same fire once and survived.

chapter 4

THE DIAGNOSIS

"Always remember that everything happens for a reason. It might not make sense now but at the right time it will."

—*Inspired Vibes*

I believe that everything you go through in life is a part of a bigger plan. A plan that is bigger than your current reality. A plan that is way beyond your ability to even imagine. You cannot see or comprehend the possibility of it having meaning or purpose while you are going through it. I am talking about when life is betting you down, to the point you are later screaming, "Lord, why me?" It only becomes clear after the storm that you realize the significance of the event. Your eyes are open, and you clearly see its connection to the next chapter of your life. Sometimes it takes days, sometimes months, and sometimes years for you to see the bigger picture. But you can rest assured that you will eventually connect the dots and see the profound connection.

The thing about extenuating circumstances is that they don't come announced. It's like one minute you're fine, and everything is okay, but the next, it all falls apart. Life doesn't come knocking at your door asking you if you're prepared to deal with misfortune. As you grow your faith, you learn that when misfortune comes knocking, the only thing you can do is surrender and tell the Lord, your will be done.

A week before my diagnosis of Corona, I was at a conference with over 5,000 teenagers hosted by an organization called HOSA. My husband was also an advisor, so we both took our students there. Coincidentally, I had severely sprained my ankle a week before the conference and was on crutches. The conference was held at the Grand Traverse Resort, a very large facility, but we stayed off-site. Due to my sprained ankle, I could not get around like I normally would. I couldn't judge an event or even work in general because I could hardly walk. Now when I think about it, I find it quite ironic. Normally, I would have run an event and been exposed to thousands of kids while at it.

However, since I was injured, I had bare minimum exposure to other people and wasn't actively around anyone for long periods of time.

We got back from the conference on a Wednesday, and the chronicles of COVID-19 were all over the news. By the end of the week, the government announced the closing of all schools in Michigan. Since I am an RN and teach a health occupations class, all my students expressed their concerns and nervousness about this unknown virus' apparent dangers. It was a daunting time for the whole world. None of us had ever heard of such a thing before, so even though I was their instructor, my knowledge about this strain of the Coronavirus was limited to the "breaking news" reports.

Chaos surrounded us. People started stocking up on sanitizers and toilet paper until the markets ran out of them. There was an actual toilet paper crisis at one point. My students were asking me what was going on and how they could keep themselves safe. I did all the research I could to communicate with them and reduce their anxiety. When we got the notice that the schools would temporarily close down until further notice, everyone was frantic. There had been viruses before different types of recessions too, but never, in my lifetime, something so scary. Never something that required the whole world to come to a halt. I explained all the preventative measures to my students, everything the World Health Organization told us about. I told them that as long as they followed universal precautions like washing their hands, covering their mouths, it would prevent the disease from spreading.

On Friday evening after work, I went out for dinner with my girlfriend and husband. It was one of my weekly rituals. I dined out every Friday with my best girlfriends. Something I truly look forward to each week. Hanging out with my girls, my fellow teaching colleagues, Lisa and Thalia, drinking a glass of wine or so, and debriefing about our week while laughing and enjoying each other's company. It amazes me how people, no matter where we go, stare at us as we thoroughly enjoy each other's company. You can see that they would join us if invited. People don't laugh anymore. I am so very grateful for my girls and sisters. I allowed my husband to hang out with us this week because Thalia could not make it.

The place was packed with people as if they knew that soon we would be deprived of our dining-out privileges. While we were out, my friend Lisa asked what we were going to do in what she referred to as the "Coronacation," the name her daughter Emily cleverly came up with, "Carona-Vacation." We thought it was hilarious at the time. We already knew we would get one week off for our spring break, but now we thought this temporary closure of schools would last another week or so. This definitely put us in the mood for a celebration.

Lisa asked a very interesting question during dinner. She asked, "What are you going to do for yourself over this extended vacation." Oddly enough, my husband recorded this conversation – something he had never done before.

She also stressed that it could not pertain to work. I'm a workaholic. All I ever think about is working on my business and non-profit, and everyone who knows me knows that, so they kept emphasizing that it could not be anything business/work-related. They told me it had to be something I do purely for myself, something to relax my overworked mind and get some rest.

My husband recorded me saying I had no idea. I could not even imagine doing anything other than catching up with some work. I could not think of anything I would rather do. I don't see my work with my business, "My School Nurse," and my non-profit, "Nurturing Wellness Group Foundation," as work. It's a calling.

Being a struggling student, myself allowed me to develop a strong passion for helping young people and schools. I love working with schools and helping them embrace strategies that support their students with mental and physical barriers. Through my non-profit, I work directly with youth and young adults to discover their greatness. I can relate to the saying, "*Do what you love, and you'll never work another day in your life.*" So, needless to say, I did not anticipate being successful with that deal.

The following Wednesday, I started to come down with a slight fever, which got worse by the minute. My joints started to hurt, and the pain was pretty uncomfortable. By the next day, Thursday, my body was sore, and there was no part of my body that was not hurting. I had severe aches in all my joints; my knees, ankles, neck, shoulders, elbows, wrists, and even my head was hurting. I felt like I got hit by a truck. I was freezing cold and shivering under my comforter.

My husband was asking me if I had come down with a cold. I told him that it was nothing but the common flu, all the while knowing I had never experienced flu that was so severe before. He checked my temperature. It was 100.5. Having watched the news too much, I was afraid about having caught COVID-19, deep in my heart. All the symptoms I was experiencing were all over the news. While I was nervous about my condition being more than just the mere flu, I did not want my husband to worry, so I kept my doubts to myself. I had all the symptoms but one. My body was aching, I had a high fever, but I did not have a cough. I was in a dilemma about whether it was Coronavirus or not.

In moments like these, you don't know where to turn. I needed answers, so I decided to call my business partner Paul, a paramedic who retired from the Detroit Fire Department. He is a part of the safety and medical staff for emergencies in Detroit and one of the smartest emergency responders I know. So, I thought, who better to ask than someone dealing with this upfront? I called Paul and explained my symptoms to him – the pain in my joints, the fever, and an unbearable aching in my body. His voice was full of worry. He told me to go to the emergency room immediately. It was late in the afternoon when I called him, so I asked if I could just go in the morning. He told me that this was nothing to play around with, it was serious and concerning, and I should not waste another second. I called my husband and informed him that we had to go to the hospital right away because Paul told me that I should not take this lightly.

We knew that many hospitals were not taking any patients with the virus symptoms through the news reports, so my husband called my sister-in-law Shanta. She worked at Beaumont Hospital. He asked her how the situation was over there. She told him they were taking patients, and I could go and get checked. When we reached the ER, there were numerous cars lined up outside of the ER. There were nurses outside wearing isolation gear, covered from head to toe with metal clipboards. I found it quite eerie since I had never seen anything like this before. I've worked in a hospital, and the ER has never looked like this. I felt like I was on a movie set, one where there is a deadly contagious virus, and everyone is scared for their life. The sad reality was that this was no movie. It was real life - the kind people write horror books about.

As we pulled into the driveway, a lady approached us and asked what brought us to the ER. I explained all my recurring symptoms to her. She asked me how long I had them. Just having that conversation with her was scary in itself because I felt like the reality of my condition was slowly sinking in. I slowly realized that everything I so deeply feared might come true. She took my name and told us to pull our car behind the cars with families living the same nightmare as my husband and me.

There were about ten cars in front of us, and the line was moving slowly. Almost an hour later, when there were about six cars ahead of us and around twenty or thirty behind us, I had to use the bathroom urgently. I told my husband to ask the nurse what we should do. He waved her over, and she told us that I could not go through the building because they were not allowing anyone inside. She further said that I would have to go through the Emergency Room entrance, to which I asked if we got out of the line, would we be allowed to come back to our spot. She nodded her head and told us that we'd have to go to the back of the line. I was getting impatient and feeling extremely frustrated. I told my husband to stay in the line and got out of the car to go to the restroom.

As I started to walk toward the front, I saw a huge yellow tent outside the emergency entrance. It was full of police officers and healthcare workers who were covered in gowns and masks. There were four people lined up, waiting to be assessed before they could enter the hospital. Suddenly, I saw an ambulance pull up with somebody they had picked up from an accident, lying on a gurney. Everywhere I looked, chaos surrounded me. I was so overwhelmed because I had no idea what to do, where to go, or even who to talk to. Everything was in shambles. The cherry on top was that my need to use the restroom only kept increasing by the minute. Luckily, one of the guys saw me and noticed the distressed look on my face. He asked me if I was okay. I told him I just really needed to use the restroom. He told me to stay put and went to call a healthcare worker to my aid. He checked my temperature, which was 100.7, and they ended up assessing me right away. They sat me down, checked my blood pressure, and asked me a few questions about the symptoms I had been experiencing. They had someone take me into the hospital Emergency Room right away.

When I walked into the emergency room, I was stunned because there was nobody. It felt odd considering how there was nothing but chaos outside, and inside, it was quite the opposite. The lady walked me to the bathroom, stood outside, and opened the door for me. She would not allow me to touch the doorknob. Once I used the restroom and came outside, she took me to a room and went outside. I was confused because she did not tell me anything and simply made me wait in this room where there was no one else.

I called my husband, who told me he was getting ready to park the car. I told him that they were not letting people come inside. He was as taken aback as I was and asked what I meant. I told him there was nobody else in the waiting room, hardly just one other patient. Since he did not believe me, I asked the nurse if he could come in. She told me to tell him to go home and that I would call him if they discharge me. Neither of us had seen this coming, but he agreed as he had no other choice and went home.

Soon the nurse came in to assess me and take my vitals, and the doctor came in shortly after her assessment. I had taken Tylenol a while ago for my pain, so it was not that bad. My fever, however, was still 100.7. The doctor told me they were out of COVID-19 test kits and that they would discharge me due to that, and I should come back if I felt worse. I found it a little absurd. I thought, if I got sick and continued to get sicker, I had no choice but to get back in that long line again, which was getting longer by the minute. I knew how terrible my condition was, and the way he handled it felt quite dismissive. He told me my symptoms were not that bad, so it was okay for me to get discharged. I was hesitant, but I did not have any choice. I started to feel frustrated and scared. I started to think about the conversation that I had with Paul earlier and his sense of urgency. I started to pray.

Just as he left, the nurse came in and was getting ready to discharge me when she looked in the drawer and found a COVID-19 test kit just lying there unattended. I remember thinking how weird it was for something so important to be lying around. It's a nasal swab that is basically a long-sterilized Q-tip in a tube. She immediately got to the doctor and told him they could conduct the test on me. By the time the doctor came back, my body had started aching again. The test was one of the most uncomfortable things I have ever experienced. The Q-tip went so far up my nose, that I felt it in my eye. I could feel it making me gag. I cannot even put into words how awful it was. I started twitching, my eyes were watering, and I felt like I could not breathe. Just when I had enough, the nurse pulled it out. As terrible as it was, thankfully, it was not too long of a procedure, and it was over soon enough.

The nurse told me it would take a day or so to get the results back, confirming if I was positive for COVID-19. She informed me that they were going to admit me due to my fever and joint pain. I was told that they would transfer me to a room as soon as one was available. You already know what happened next. The test came back positive. It was what felt like the beginning of the end for me. Alone and afraid and defiantly one of those moments, where I cried out, "Lord, why me?"

chapter 5

HOSPITAL (PART 1)

"You may not control all the events that happen to you, but you can decide not to be reduced by them."

—*Maya Angelou*

I am a bit of a control freak. Okay, I said it; I can be extremely demanding, especially when I think I have total control over the outcome. I do not mind working hard and putting the time in. I would say that I am a little compulsive but quite reasonable. I know how to work with people. I have a high regard for building sustainable relationships. I value friendship and am very intentional about maintaining a level of mutual respect. For most of my adult life, I have embraced these values. I truly believe that if I work hard, treat people right, and stay focused on my ambitions, everything will work out for my good. I believe that the Lord used the last few years to show me how I am not in control.

Over the last couple of years, no matter how well I scheduled, strategized, planned, and treated people, something horrible would happen. It was not like I had a dark cloud over my head but more like doors being slammed in my face (figuratively, of course). It was like an unambiguous message saying, "Stop and pay attention." This is the best way I can describe it. It became extremely apparent that I was not in control.

It has been a tough few years, to say the least. It seemed like every time I thought I had everything under control, something crazy would happen. When I say crazy, I don't mean everyday miss-happenstances. I mean all-out, unexplainable encounters that centered around my health. For example, I love to sing. When my children were young, I used to sing throughout the house while cleaning, cooking, and caring for my children. I would sing gospel songs, nursery rhymes, and anything. My boys often share fond memories of their private mom concerts.

One day, my youngest son Terrance told me that my voice sounded different. I did not make anything of it, but shortly after that day, I started to have severe pain in the front of my neck. It was so severe that my husband rushed me to the hospital on two different occasions. Each time I arrived at the ER, the pain would disappear. Confused by this phenomenon, the ER doctor ordered an ultrasound of my neck. To make a very long story short, I was diagnosed with thyroid cancer that had metastasized to my parathyroid. Thank God we got it diagnosed in time, and it was successfully removed and treated with radiation.

The most shocking and unbelievable thing about this is that thyroid cancer is asymptomatic (without symptoms). Changes in your voice and pain in your throat are not normally seen with this type of cancer. Fortunately for me, after I was rushed to the hospital the second time due to the pain in my neck and treated, I never experienced that pain again. This was one of my many "stop and pay attention" encounters. All of 2019, I struggled with severe nerve pain shooting down my right arm. It was horrific. I would cry myself to sleep. It made it extremely difficult to type and work on my business, but I did not let it stop me. I used ice, heat, and pretty much anything I could take to help relieve the pain, but nothing helped me. My husband connected me to Dr. Rosenberg, a doctor with whom he had worked. I was able to receive some relief through a stellate ganglion block injection in my neck. I receive this injection every three to four weeks. It was a lot, but it was worth it.

I tested positive for COVID-19 on March 19, 2020. Initially, the news was shocking, but its seriousness did not settle in until my health started to decline. From the time I was admitted to the hospital, I existed in a heavy fog. Most of the things that happened to me feel like a hazy memory.

Soon after I was admitted, my oxygen started to drop, and my condition worsened. I remember once I was a little more stable, everything slowly started to sink in. There's nothing beautiful about trauma. It's ugly, painful, horrible, and what feels like the end of the world. The outcome of agony is what you could call beautiful because pain creates warriors; it makes people stronger.

However, my reality left me with a different perspective at that time. It's when you look at your reflection in the mirror at 3 a.m., cry your eyes out, and tell yourself it's going to be okay. It's when you clench your fists and let tears silently fall down your cheeks when all you want to do is scream out loud about how unfair life is. It's when you feel like the ground is splitting beneath your feet and you don't know what to hold on to save yourself from drowning. It's a dark alley where the only light you have is hope. I hoped that things would get better. I remembered a scripture in God's Word, "But those who hope in the Lord will renew their strength. They will soar on wings like eagles; they will run and not grow weary; they will walk and not be faint." Isaiah 40:31. When you need encouragement and refreshment for your soul, you will find much comfort when you turn to scriptures from the Old and New Testaments of the Bible. God's word allowed me to embrace the fact that this pain was temporary, that no matter how hard it may be, as long as I was still alive, there was hope.

Being in isolation, away from all those people I love so dearly, I realized how I put so many people at risk by interacting with them. More than anything, I was embarrassed. I started texting everyone I had met a few days before being admitted. The list was too long and instilled a great deal of guilt into me. Having gotten my hair done a few days ago, one of my first few texts was to my hairdresser Simone, letting her know about my condition so she could take precautionary measures. I called all my girlfriends and some of my co-workers too. I could not stop feeling mortified for having exposed my loved ones to this virus.

It's an overwhelming feeling, thinking you could be the reason for someone's sickness and that there is a good chance you were not careful enough simply because you did not take enough precautions. When something of such gravity happens, we often fail to take it seriously because we somehow think there's no reason for it to happen to us. I remember praying to God that I don't become the reason for someone's illness, for someone who came in contact with me to get COVID too.

My heart was heavy and full of fear. Just a few days ago, I was telling my kids at school to take precautionary measures. I told them how to prevent themselves from getting it. Yet, here I was, lying helplessly in an isolated room, worrying I had put numerous lives at risk. Oddly enough, from the moment I was hospitalized, my condition started progressively getting worse over just 24 hours. I went from walking into the emergency room with a fever, aching joints, and an unsettling fear of what may be the point where I could hardly catch my breath. I was being given oxygen through a nasal cannula. My condition worsened to the point where I had a hard time going to the bathroom because that meant taking the oxygen off.

Everything was chaotic. I went from one end of the spectrum to the other in a relatively short period of time. I did not even have the energy to get out of bed. I remember how every once in a while, someone would come into my room covered from head to toe in protective gear to take my chest X-Ray or draw my blood. I had never experienced loneliness so up close where I had nobody to talk to and share my fears with. I did not even have enough energy to turn the TV on. I just sat in silence, not even consumed with thoughts. The sacredness of human touch felt like a luxury I had taken for granted all my life. As I lay there, helpless and drained, God decided to bless me by providing me peace. I had learned to pay attention, so I knew that it was His handy work. As I mentioned before, my sister-in-law Shanta is an RN and worked on the same floor that I was on, she would come and check up on me when she could and keep my family updated with my progress, but at the same time, she could only be around me for so long. Nonetheless, knowing that she was there gave me peace.

Gradually, I was becoming a depiction of a zombie. I lost my sense of smell and stopped eating and drinking too. I was given many different medicines, and none of them seemed to improve my health even a bit. Of course, a great reason for that was that this virus was new. When someone has cancer, the doctors know how to deal with it, but this was a virus that had just been discovered, one that was quite literally wiping a great chunk of the population out. It was a foreign territory, even for the world's best doctors.

My husband told me that the doctor wanted me to use the incentive spirometer to help increase my lung capacity. Every time I used it, I would cough aggressively, and it hurt every part of my body so much that I stopped using it altogether. My husband and son Travis felt as helpless as I did. They would call me multiple times and ask me to use the spirometer because otherwise, my lungs would get full of fluids. In addition to that, I slowly started to get more and more confused and disoriented. I was physically there in that room, but mentally, I had checked out. When I hear from my sister-in-law or husband about how I had become, it feels eerie. They tell me that I did not watch TV or listen to music. I would lie still in bed, trying to breathe.

I vaguely remember how she would come to me multiple times, telling me that I needed to breathe and that I could not give up. My husband would call me and beg me to eat something. At one point, I told him I ate some French fries, and he was overjoyed. He told me to order some more for the next day, but my appetite was gone, and I had to tell him that I could not eat them. The point being, everything was happening at a fast pace. Life was coming crashing down like a bullet train at full speed. I could not process anything. I could not smell or taste anything. I just lay there restless and defeated.

After three long days of progressively getting worse, the doctor came in and told me that my pulse oximeter reading was extremely low and not improving. A normal SpO2 is at least 95%, while mine was 79%, and I was on oxygen. He told me that I had developed pneumonia in my left lung, and nothing was working, so my best bet was to go on a ventilator. Being an RN, I was familiar with how people went on vents. I had seen patients go on them, but I had never been on one myself. I was really scared and somewhat in shock too. I could not have seen any of this happen a mile away. I asked the doctor what the prognosis was, meaning if I was going to go on a vent, what would the risks implicate. The doctor's answer gave me goosebumps. He told me that there was a good chance I may not come off it. I could simply not fathom what he said. The fact that I could die hit me hard.

Death doesn't knock at your door or ask you if you're ready to leave. It just breaks the door and forces you to leave, regardless of whether you're prepared or not. Honestly, I don't think any of us can ever prepare ourselves for death. I could not bring myself to call my husband and tell him that there was a possibility for the love of his life to be gone forever.

In movies, when you see something like that, there's ominous music, and the screen goes dark. In my life's reality, though, it was nothing like that. I was scared and felt helpless. Narrating a true story, decreasing the trauma you felt at that moment into words, has always baffled me. *How do you tell a story and explain an emotion when you don't even have the right words to describe it?* I picked up the phone, trying to muster the courage to call my husband, but ended up dialing my sister-in-law Robin's number instead. She is a nurse practitioner and lives in Ohio with her husband, a neurologist. I remember the first thing I asked her was if I could die. I was losing my mind and needed someone to tell me that everything would be okay. I needed reassurance.

Robin went silent. That silence was louder than anything I had ever heard. It was heart-wrenching. As she started to cry on the other side of the phone, her husband Mike took the phone from her and started to talk to me. While I have no memory of what he said to me, how he gave me hope, or the reassuring words he said to me, I just remember that my heart was at peace by the time we were done talking. They told me they loved me and hung up the phone, after which I felt like everything was going to be okay, and I was ready to go on the vent.

I'm not quite sure about when I called my husband and told him everything. I am pretty sure he spoke with the doctor directly. I hardly remember any of it, but he kept asking me if I was sure about my decision. He asked me if I knew the risks and was willing to take them. He even said that I was nonchalant about the whole thing. I took a small gasp of air as I reassured him that I could not breathe and had no choice. He told me that he was really worried, whereas I sounded as if I just wanted relief. It was as though I was sure that I'd be seeing him again. I ended the call by saying, "I love you and I will see you later."

Coincidentally, my brother's best friend also tested positive for COVID, and he was in the room next to mine. Shanta looked after both of us while dealing with the emotional stress of watching two people she cared about struggling for their lives. She called the respiratory team and the anesthesiologist, and they put me on the vent.

Thinking back to that time gives me chills down my spine because I went from teaching my students about this newfound virus to being wrapped in its wrath. I had no control over what was happening to me.

The doctors had no idea how I was going to get any better. I was alive but broken and had somewhat accepted that this might be the end. I had a good run, and now it was over. I remember thinking, 'I have so much I want to do.' There was so much I hadn't done. I was not ready to go. "Your will be done," was my last prayer.

If there is one thing I learned, it's never to take anything in life for granted. We often spend a good chunk of our time being upset over petty things, forgetting that everything can change within a split second. We should know better than to be careless and take all the precautionary measures we're asked to. Life is the definition of the unexpected. Just when you think everything's perfect and finally get in your comfort zone, it drags you out of it and reminds you that comfort, worldly happiness is temporary. Nevertheless, they don't last, and there's no such thing as a perfect life. Instead of hoping for things to never go wrong, I learned to cherish every moment - the good, the bad, and the ugly. I've learned to look for the lesson in the hard times. "Stop and pay attention," He is trying to tell you something, teach you a lesson, or even prepare you for something. Now when hard times come, I think, wow, Lord, what are You getting me ready for? I am not in control. I am definitely aware of that now, but I have peace because I know who is in control.

chapter 6

HOSPITAL (PART 2)

"Sometimes the best thing you can do is not think, not wonder, not imagine, not obsess. Just Breathe and have Faith that everything will work out for the best."

—*Inspire Positive Soul Sensations*

Sometimes, God says no, and you have no choice but to accept the consequences. You can give up or choose to fight. You always have a choice regardless of the circumstances. I have learned that focusing on the things you don't have control over is what makes most situations worse. For example, if someone misrepresents you, you may instantly feel hurt and betrayed by the lies being spread about you. You have no control over what was said or how others react to the lie. But you do have control over how you respond.

You can state your case and give everyone a piece of your mind who believed them, or you can choose to look for the lesson. Maybe, your co-worker treats you like crap, and you truly have not done anything to deserve it. Sure, you can treat them the same way and attempt to make their life as miserable as they have made yours. But again, you do have control over how you respond. Maybe you are harboring unforgiveness and you justify your unethical behavior choices by your feelings of unforgiveness.

You must remember to look for the things you can control. I have found that when I keep experiencing the same type of situation over and over again, I must be missing the lesson. As I lay in the hospital lifeless, I had no thoughts. I was not angry. I was not even resentful or scared at that point, maybe because it was an unfamiliar place for me - no emotions at all. When you can't breathe, it is extremely hard to ponder over anything but breathing. I held up my white flag and surrendered. The respiratory team and the anesthesiologist were called. They put me on the vent. "Your will be done," was my last prayer. Although I had never surrendered to this magnitude, this was a familiar feeling – a feeling of peace.

When I first got married, I was a pistol, to say the least. Growing up in the '80s, I was my own woman, with role models like Whitney Houston, Janet Jackson, Madonna, and Cyndi Lauper. I was into fashion, big hair, and an attitude. Janet Jackson's song, "Control," was my anthem. With my icons and mom, who happens to be my biggest cheerleader, she was egging me on to take charge of my destiny and be that "Material Girl" that Madonna sang about. Live a rich and affluent life rather than romance and relationships. But marriage was different. I emphasized marriage and the wedding, not so much on the relationship.

I was determined that I would be married and have two children and an important job that I could dress up for and make a difference. Yes, I wanted to be a working woman and the perfect housewife. It was going great for a while but quickly became a bit out of order. I was so stressed out because I did not know how to turn off my new work ethic. I strived to maintain perfection. I learned very quickly that God's design for marriage was perfect. I resisted His instruction for wives to submit to their husbands due to my warped interpretation of God's word. Yet, it *never* suggests that one spouse is more important than the other. Instead, when a Christian husband and wife learn how God has wired them to complement each other in mutual submission, they reflect the love that exists between Christ and His Bride.

I was blind to this perfect design at first, and when I finally discovered this wisdom, I was on the verge of losing my marriage. But God intervened and opened my eyes. I held up my white flag and surrendered. I must admit I had to surrender a few times before I truly submitted. But when I did, my stress reduced and I felt protected, safe, and an overwhelming feeling of peace. The feeling of summiting to God's will can be extremely scary at first. Like dangling from the top of a building and struggling to hold on. Choosing to struggle and fight and cry is defiantly an option. But when you let go and He catches you, all your worries, anxiety, and stress miraculously disappear.

When a person cannot breathe on their own or maintain an open airway, they may require intubation and the use of a ventilator. Intubation is the process of inserting a breathing tube through the mouth and into the airway. A ventilator, also known as a respirator or breathing machine, is a medical device that provides oxygen through the breathing tube. The ventilator was breathing for me while my lungs healed. The breathing tube was connected to the ventilator. The ventilator pushed air into my lungs to deliver a breath, then allowed the air to come back out, just as the lungs would do if they were able to.

While I was on the vent, I remember everything. It was like being in a different world. Although I know now that my experience was a dream, it was very vivid and felt real. I don't remember the order of my dreams, but I know I was extremely afraid and confused. I remember being in an abandoned old hospital with old raggedy medical equipment. It was dirty and dingy hospital curtains hanging from the ceiling and dividing the patient's areas. My bed was low to the ground, and my arms were restrained with a rope. As I peeked through the deteriorating and torn openings in the curtains, I could see that I was in a basement where old beds were stacked against one another, upside down and broken. I saw different people in the beds. There were ladies that I saw dressed in dirty white scrubs. They may have been nurses. I had on a dirty, dingy blue gown. I was so confused. I had no idea where I was and how I got there.

I thought that I had been kidnapped and was being trafficked. I felt like the kidnappers kept me drugged most of the time. All of those memories are very hazy for me, but I thought I was in Mexico. Staying on the vent had some serious effects on my mental health. I felt like my dreams were connected to my reality. I was suffering to find a way out of my head.

Most of my thoughts and dreams were connected to some of my experiences before my hospitalization. I was able to make the connection when I was discharged from the hospital. Prior to being admitted, I was having a lot of issues with one of my co-workers and was very disturbed. I was being given a really tough time and got very overwhelmed with the entire ordeal. While I was going through all of that, I was suddenly diagnosed with COVID-19. It felt like going from a frying pan into the fire. Everything went from bad to worse for me.

While I was struggling with my co-worker, I started listening to Joyce Myers, an evangelist woman minister. I started listening to her Bible study every day on my way to work. Every time her Bible study was over, I would pray and ask God to speak to my heart and soften my spirit toward my co-worker. Although I was extremely angry, I wanted to remain true to my character and not lose my integrity. I wanted to be like Christ, be angry but not sin. Needless to say, I failed miserably, but God knows my heart. I know now that this situation kept me in God's word. I was so frustrated because I had left my job after 20 years, only to start a new job in a new place that I felt disconnected, mistreated, and lonely.

After Joyce Myers Bible study, she would play an advertisement about her evangelism ministry. She would always have testimonies from young women being saved from sex trafficking. Now when I think about it, I realize my dreams and thoughts were connected to these commercials. It was all just stuck in my head, but it felt so real. While I was on the vent, I thought I was being trafficked.

I saw myself in the city of Detroit at one time, in some facility inside an old building, sitting in a chair. I was telling the people in that facility that I had escaped the traffickers and that I needed them to get in touch with my family. I told them that I needed my family to know I was safe. People kept telling me that they would call my family for me, but it felt like time was just moving very slowly. I remember staring out the window at the hospital and seeing my sister-in-law Shanta from afar. I could recognize her eyes, but my vision would be blocked by what I thought was a scarf, but it was a mask in reality.

Shanta even told me that while I was in the ICU, she would come by the room to pray for me as she watched me through the window. I would open my eyes and look at her. I also remember looking at her in my dreams and thinking, "Why don't you just come in here and get me? Why are you letting these people keep me in this room? Come get me!" I even remember saying to some lady, "That is Shanta. She has such a sweet face. Why can't she just take me home?" I was clearly dreaming. Lol. Nevertheless, seeing her, I did feel safe. Her eyes told me that everything was going to be alright.

There was another dream where I would see myself in a park surrounded by beautiful green grass. I also recall seeing this humongous, colorful ball playing really loud music. It was just sitting in the middle of this field of dark green grass. Bright blues, yellows, and orange abstract designs decorated its outside. The music was getting me closer. I could hear various sorts of music at the same time. I could hear Japanese, tribal music, and whatnot.

I do not know if that makes any sense, but that is what I dreamed. I remember searching for an opening in the ball. I found a very narrow opening. I was very curious as I stepped inside. I heard a voice telling me to strap myself in. Once I strapped myself inside the ball, the music got a lot louder, and the ball started rolling. I heard a lot of busyness, muffled voices, and buzzing. The ball kept rolling, and there was a continuous beeping sound that was driving me crazy. I remember crying out for all of it to stop, yelling that I was done and that I just wanted to get out. I heard someone saying, "You are okay." They were trying to calm me down and repeatedly told me that I could come out. Finally, everything stopped.

While I was on the ventilator, my sister-in-law Robin stayed in constant contact with my husband. She, along with Shanta, helped him stay sane. Robin is a Nurse Practitioner and was researching the impact of a ventilator. On my tenth day of being on the vent, she shared an article with my husband. It talked about the outcomes of being on the vent for too long. The article indicated that surviving time on a ventilator sometimes leads to complications, and lung function might not fully recover in COVID-19 patients.

At that time, The Associated Press reported in April that New York City officials said 80% of patients on ventilators there had died. "The longer you are on a ventilator, the less likely you will ever come off that ventilator," Cuomo said in an April briefing.

The complications associated with coming off a ventilator can differ based on how long a patient was on the machine. Patients with severe cases of COVID-19, as I was, can also experience failures of other organs, such as their kidneys, and these can have long-term consequences.

"Coming off a ventilator is the beginning of the end," Dr. Patrick Maher, a pulmonary medicine doctor with Mount Sinai who's been treating COVID-19 patients in the hospital's intensive care units, told Business Insider.

The heavy doses of sedation and blood pressure medications used to keep patients stable on the ventilators as their lung recovery could come with side effects. One is delirium, doctors told Business Insider in April. It's not easy to be sedated for that long.

The aftereffects of being on the vent scared everyone. As I mentioned before, Robin created a prayer line for me that I believe had a major impact on my recovery. The nurses indicated that I was responding to their prayers and fighting to breathe on my own. The breathing machine was beeping and buzzing and going crazy from me fighting the vent as I struggled to breathe. My youngest son was very upset by the noise and asked if they could stop because I did not like it. But the nurse reassured him that I was okay.

They held a second prayer session as the nurse held the phone to my ear. Shortly after that, my readings became more stable. I was able to be weaned off the ventilator. The ventilator was removed once I could breathe on my own. They pulled the tube out of my throat, and I started to wake up gradually.

I remember being in a dark and dingy room. I smelled smoke and could see soot flying around me. Both my arms were restrained. I remember being afraid. No one looked familiar. I thought I was still in Mexico because I heard the Mexican dogs barking. Ok, I was on a lot of drugs. I was awake, and each time someone walked by my window and looked in, I closed my eyes and acted like I was asleep. I was trying to hide from them because I thought I had been kidnapped. The nurse did not know that I was awake because they were busy doing something in the corner of the room. At first, I thought that I was dreaming, but what I am about to tell you next actually did happen. Shanta verified my encounter after speaking with the ICU nurse.

I saw the nurse walking by the window and closed my eyes since I was trying to hide the fact that I was awake. I figured that if they did not know that I was awake and I behaved well, they would not punish me. There were two doors to my room that they kept me in - one right after the other. I noticed that they never left out of the second door and never used a key to enter the second door. I thought if I could get to the door, I had a chance to escape. I tried to loosen the restraints from my hands, and eventually, I was able to wiggle my hands out. It took me a while to get out of bed onto the floor and crawl to the door. I wanted to escape because I thought that they were going to torture me. I was not going out without a fight.

The nurse came into the room from the other door and saw me trying to escape. She rushed in and started pointing at me, crawling on the floor and screaming, "COVID-19! COVID-19!" I perceived her words as, "Covert Operation! Covert Operation!" I thought that I was being trafficked, and they had caught me while trying to escape.

A group of nurses gathered around me as I frantically tried to reach the door. I was desperately trying to break free. All of them were trying to get a hold of me. They were trying to calm me down by telling me that everything was okay, but I kept fighting, crying, and pleading for them to let me go. Finally, I locked eyes with one of the nurses. She must have seen the sheer terror in my eyes. She exclaimed, "You don't know where you are." I kept screaming and screaming, and then she kept telling me that I was in a hospital. She said, "Honey, you are in the hospital. You are okay." Trying her best to calm me down, the nurse told me that she would call someone for me. I pleaded with her to call my mom, and so she did. I remembered my mom's number. She has had the same number for over fifty (50) years. They put my mom on speaker for me to talk to her.

My mom said, "Terri, are you okay?"

I anxiously asked her if she knew where I was.

She said, "You are in the hospital."

I exclaimed, "No! They moved me from there!"

My mother once again told me, "We know where you are. You are in the hospital."

The craziest thing about this entire ordeal was that my mother later told me that she could hear me clearly, and she immediately recognized me. I remember myself screaming and hollering, but I had not been able to talk for weeks due to the ventilator tube down my throat. They had just removed the tube. My voice was completely hoarse. I still do not get how I was able to scream and get out of my bed. I could not even walk because I had been on the vent for nearly 15 days. I was bedridden. Hence, I suffered muscle atrophy. I still wonder how in the world I was able to scream and get out of my bed. It is amazing how your adrenaline can impact your mind and body in such a way that you can do impossible things.

Once they finally calmed me down and got me back into bed, I came to the realization that I was indeed in the hospital. The nurse tried to explain to me what had happened, but I had no memory. The only person I remember was my mother. I did not even remember that I was a married woman with two children. I just could not recall anything. Once they finally assured me that I was fine, I was afraid of going to sleep because I thought I would die or would not be able to wake up. So, I just remember being in the ICU, terrified to fall asleep. I recall everything being dingy. I continued to smell smoke and I still thought that I was in Mexico. This was a very confusing time for me. I could smell something burning. I thought they were burning all of the sheets and whatever was being used for us Covid patients.

I remember being so fearful of going to sleep that I would start praying to God, asking him not to take me away. I thought I was going to aspirate because I kept throwing up. They were not feeding me orally, but I kept throwing up all this liquid. I felt that if I went to sleep, I would aspirate, and they would not be able to save me. That is one of the reasons I was unable to sleep. I was pleading with God to help me, and if my time had come, help me accept it. I just felt it in my spirit that I was going to die. Although I had forgotten about my husband and kids, and all I remembered was having a mother, I felt like I had a lot to do in this world, and I did not want to go. I never felt alone. I felt like I was speaking with God, like He was in the room with me, even though there were barely any people in my room, as what I had was extremely contagious. Nobody wanted to stay too long in my room, but I never felt like I was alone.

I always felt like someone else was also there with me. You know that feeling when you are lying down in bed, and you just feel someone's presence in the room, but when you look around, no one is there. I felt that presence. I was not afraid of this presence or anything, but I knew someone was in that room with me, and I felt like I was being protected. Someone whose presence I could only feel was taking up half of the stress from me. It was as if someone was sharing this burden with me. If I found myself unable to bear the stress, this invisible presence would take it away from me and make me feel protected and safe. The more I prayed, the less anxious I felt. I finally gave up, placed my trust in the Lord, and went to sleep. I had a feeling of peace engulf me from that day on. Upon waking up the next day, I realized something and was exhilarated. I was alive. I was alive and breathing.

After that, the doctors wanted to see if I could move around to be discharged from the ICU. I was visited by two physical therapists who asked me if I could get up. I said, "Sure, why not?"

The next moment, I literally got up. Although two people were giving me some support to get up, I made it to the chair in front of my bed. They were shocked to see me make such progress just coming off a vent. When my vitals started doing better, they reduced my supplemental oxygen level. I could move a bit more on my own. I was later transferred to another unit. I had been stuck in that room for so long that when they put me in a wheelchair and pushed me down the hall, I felt like I was running. My memory was starting to return, and I wanted to rush to the room. It was because my husband had sent my phone to my room for me to FaceTime with him. Upon arriving in my room, I just remember the room being neat and clean. The sun was shining in the window, the deep redwood floor was sparkling, and everything was bright and perfectly pleasant. No more soot flying around and no more smoke smell. I swear I heard birds chirping. I felt so happy that I just broke down crying and kept thanking God.

My voice was still very low, so the nurses did not know what I was saying. They began to worry until another nurse told them that I was praying. I was crying and raising my arms, praising the Lord and thanking Him for saving me. They finally got me into the room and gave me my phone to call my husband. I remember as soon as my husband saw my face, he burst into tears. Both of us kept on crying until my nurse entered the room and encouraged me to calm down. She was worried about my oxygen. She and the nurse aide asked me if I knew how long I had been in the hospital. I told them that I think it was two to three days. I remember the two of them looked at each other and said, "No, honey, you have been here for over 20 days. You were on the vent for 15 days." I was shocked. My husband was still on the phone. He confirmed what they said.

The nurses actually tried their best to take care of me. However, they did not enter the room that often. I could feel how concerned they were for my well-being. They were all really nice to me and accommodated me in every way possible. I remember being in the room all by myself most of the time, feeling really isolated and weak. I could hardly walk, but I refused to stop trying. I started getting depressed with the state of our world. Talking to my husband, I found out what was happening all around the world.

I almost felt like I was in a twilight zone. I felt like I was in a parallel universe. I remembered the world in a different way before going to the hospital, and now it was a completely different planet. I learned about all the people who died. It really made me feel overwhelmed. It was all still sinking in. I had been out of contact with the world for weeks, and it felt like the world was a totally different place.

I was desperately trying to get well so that I could go home. I was weak, but I was trying to push myself. My hair was all over my head. I lost so much weight that I felt like a little ragdoll. I did not want to worry the staff, so I slowly got myself up to the bathroom. I was sitting on the toilet and could not get up. I became very emotional because I was extremely weak and dizzy. I was scared and began to cry. I pulled the nurse cord, and the nurse rushed in. I was so torn and upset. I wanted my mom and could not catch my breath.

The nurse stood in front of me and placed my head on her stomach. She started raking my hair with her fingers and patted the back of my head. She tried hard to console me. I remember holding on to her and crying. It had been a while since I had physical contact with anyone. The most I ever got to interact with someone over those weeks was when someone would give me a shot or something. I felt like I needed my mom and family. I needed someone's touch. When the nurse touched me, I felt like this nightmare was almost over. There was an overwhelming feeling within me that made me believe that everything would be okay.

Shortly after my bathroom encounter, I started to hear these announcements over the P.A. regulatory, alert respiratory to room five;

respiratory, respiratory." I then understood that these types of alerts meant that somebody was in respiratory distress, and I assumed it was due to COVID. It reminded me of what I went through a few weeks earlier when my oxygen level had bottomed out. I started to think about the fact that I know what that felt like. 'I'm at the end of my journey of being in the hospital, and this person is just starting,' I thought to myself every time I heard that alert. I would pray for the patient, their family, and the staff.

The more I prayed, the stronger I became. It gave me a purpose. I felt like this was my assignment. I knew the journey that they were getting ready to embark on, so I was very specific in my prayers because I knew what they were going to go through. I stopped asking why me, Lord, and accepted my new assignment to pray. I also started praying for the staff, and any time that anyone would come in the room, I asked them if I could pray for them. Oddly enough, they really couldn't hear me pray because my voice was still really low, but I would still pray for them.

I was so grateful that I had survived, which so many others did not. My husband told me how many people were dying, and I started watching the news on TV. It was just a very humbling but eerie feeling when I heard that entire families were dying. It was all just so too much to truly comprehend, and I just had thoughts about why God chose to spare me. Why was I still here?

While I was in the hospital going through my struggles, my family also had a rough time coping with what I was going through, in addition to the state of our world. With my health declining and the uncertainty of my survival, they were also bombarded by the world's events. The entire world was feeling the impact of the lockdown, and the death tolls were devastating. I'm sure most people hugged their loved ones a little tighter during this time. I can only imagine how scary it was for my family, knowing that their wife, mother, daughter, and sister were fighting for her life from the same unknown disease that was causing so much unrest throughout our world.

My beloved family went through the pain of learning about neighbors, classmates, church members, and others dying around them. They got to know stories about mothers losing their children and husbands, a child losing both of his parents, a sister losing her brothers - so much hardship and loss. They would even hear stories about how families could not conduct a funeral for their loved ones who passed away because that could further spread the virus. I was not the only one suffering. They had to go through a lot of stress and anxiety too.

My mother, in her '80s, was quarantined in her home because she had existing medical conditions and was at risk of getting infected. While she had to be cut off from everyone, my sister Semon could not even take care of her because she was quarantined in her own home. Just like anyone's mother, my mother was extremely worried about me. It is not normal for anyone to find out that a deadly virus has infected their child. Many friends and people from our church checked on her and prayed with her. I was very grateful for them all when I learned how everyone supported my mom and my entire family. I am so blessed to have such a wonderful community of friends and family.

Everyone connected to me was struggling. They saw the death toll numbers going up every day. My husband said that he started getting severely concerned. At one point, the numbers were so high that they did not have anywhere to put the bodies. All the morgues were full. They had to bring in refrigerated trucks to store the bodies because they did not have any space. They even had to use civic centers as makeshift hospitals to support the overflow of patients. Not only did they suffer from having insufficient space, but they were also running out of important equipment like masks, gloves, and ventilators. My husband had worked in the medical field, and through his contacts, he would find out how haphazard the situation was. At one point, things in New York started getting so much out of hand that the government had to bring in navy ships to support the virus outbreak.

My husband was also fearful because I was one of the people affected by the virus' first wave. At that time, doctors did not know how to deal with COVID-19, and the survival rate was very low. It was being perceived as a death sentence when someone was diagnosed with it. We lost many members of our community.

I felt really bad, and I still do, thinking about how my entire family was struggling during this difficult time. My husband tried his best to keep everyone in the loop. My son Travis and husband would take turns calling the hospital and checking on me when I was in the ICU. He even created a group text on my phone with all my friends, family, and co-workers. He would provide everyone with an update on my health. While I was on the vent, my friends and co-workers would call and pray with him. He shared how he was moved after receiving a call from one of my mentees Robin, and she prayed with him. Our dear friend Deacon Smith even called from Hawaii just to provide words of encouragement and pray with my husband.

Our church started a daily prayer line. It provided a great deal of comfort for my husband. Having good friends helped us a lot. It gave my family strength. Even the principal from my school and different acquaintances would make sure to keep a check on my husband. My sister, friends, and so many people prayed for us during this time. It was humbling to learn about so many people taking the time to call, text, pray, send cards, and reach out to my children.

God moved people, and I greatly appreciated the enormous outpour of love. It had been difficult for me to accept help from others. I love being on the giving end instead of the receiving one. But I realize now that it's impossible to do life without help and support from others. We need each other. When people walked by my door and waved at me, I felt a sense of warmth and gratitude. We need a human touch. We can't survive without it. We only need to choose to accept support from others. It's a simple choice for some and darn right agonizing for others. When we resist, we may be missing out on our blessing. A stranger stroked my head and provided just what I needed when I needed it. I freely accepted her kindness and knew she was a gift from God.

chapter 7

RECOVERY

"It has been said that time heals all wounds. The truth is that time does not heal anything. It merely passes. It is what we do during the passing of the time that helps or hinders the healing process."

—*Jay Marshall*

When I was discharged from the hospital, it was all very surreal for me. I was there for such a long time that my mind was still playing tricks on me. Just being in the hallway outside my room felt weird. So, when they came to get me, I harbored a mixed feeling of joy and apprehension as I left my room.

I couldn't have imagined what was waiting for me outside my door, let alone outside the hospital. As the transporter rolled me out of my room, I felt a rush of fresh cool air whisking past me. I immediately felt a chill, and I could see goosebumps on my arms. People were standing on both sides of the hallway, right up to the elevator, and everybody was cheering and looking in my direction. They were all clapping so hard. Since I was still a little bit disoriented, I started clapping too. I didn't know what was happening around me. I was completely baffled and asked the transporter why everyone was clapping. She smiled and said, they are clapping for you. Why I asked, and she replied by saying they are congratulating you on recovery. They were really happy that, upon spending 29 days in battle, I was finally returning home. You are extremely lucky, she said. *'Luck had nothing to do with it,'* I thought.

That is when everything fell into place for me. My entire ordeal and my reception in the hallway all made sense now. As they walked me out, I saw my husband sitting in the car, waiting for me. We both just looked at each other. It was almost a month since we had set eyes on each other, and each of us was drinking in the image of the other. The last time he saw me was when he had dropped me off in the ER at the hospital, and now, here he was, picking me up.

I did not know how to respond. I was scared that I was dreaming and did not want to wake up. I was strapped in. He looked nervous. He looked at me like I was unreal. I felt like we had both survived a major ordeal, like a plane crash or something. We were both pretty quiet and didn't really speak a word. I remember taking my shoes off and putting my feet on the dashboard. I had mismatched socks on that my son gave me a few months before I went into the hospital. They were soft and warm, and the sun was shining bright on my feet. My husband was holding and rubbing my hand. I started crying as reality was slowly setting in, and I realized it all. My husband, on the other hand, was smiling. I simply thought I was in a dream because, as I said, I was still a little bit disoriented.

The lockdown was still in place, people were still quarantined, and the entire state was shut down. There were no cars or people outside as we made our way home. It all looked like a mirage utterly fictional. I couldn't recognize half of the stuff or places we passed by, which made me even more paranoid. My mind kept taking me back to the assumption of being kidnapped. I tried to fight those feelings and shared my concerns with my husband. He immediately assured me that I was safe, and I calmed down, but I remained anxious and unsure.

When we finally arrived home, I was pleasantly surprised to see that my husband had arranged a surprise for me. Everyone from my family, friends, neighbors, and people from my church were there, parked along the side of the street. As our car pulled up, everybody started blowing their horns. Others might think that it was a cacophony, but to my ears, it was absolutely wonderful. It was music, the likes of which I had never heard before.

This was when I started recognizing that I was still alive and well. In reality, this was not some peculiar dream. The honking cars and the people yelling and waving at me was what it took for me to embrace that I was back. There were around 25 people welcoming me, and that was when I understood that I was going to survive. I was going to make it. This was one of the best welcomes I've ever had. I was so grateful to see all the familiar faces, and it was long overdue.

Once we reached our home, I tried my best to get back to my life, but it was easier said than done. I didn't know how many changes I had been through. Only when I started regaining some normalcy that I understand it all. I could hardly walk; my gait had changed a lot. My legs felt extremely heavy. I spent so much time in the hospital room that everything felt weird to me. The openness, the multiple rooms, the fresh air, it was all very difficult to accept. It kept making me dizzy. There was simply so much stimulation that I couldn't handle it at all. I felt most comfortable in my room, with the door closed.

Then there was that incessant coughing. I was having coughing fits, which took all the fight out of me. I was still on oxygen, so I couldn't get around much. My husband had to help me enter the house when we arrived. Our house is tri-level, so there were a lot of steps. I felt like a visitor in my own home.

As I spent more and more time at home, I started realizing how sick I actually was. I mean, I already knew it in the hospital, but there everything was available to support me and keep me safe. Here, even though I was in my own environment, things were extremely difficult. I had a very hard time breathing. It was hard for me to take a single deep breath. No matter what I did, it seemed that I was always out of breath. When I did breathe a little, I would start coughing. I was coughing so much that there was a constant ache in my chest. My chest hurt, and so did my head, legs, and everything else.

As if that wasn't enough, I was having a hard time remembering things. I had some of my memories, but some of them I completely lost and didn't know whether I would ever get them back or not. My husband would come to me and inform me that certain people called me or checked up on me. He would tell me that Mr. Donaldson and Mr. Evans called me, and I would look at him with a puzzled look on my face. Although I nodded and smiled, was I supposed to know these people? Who were they? How did I know them? All these questions and many more were flooding my mind and worsening my already delicate state. I know that I had worked hard on my mind. I recalled that I had a learning disability, and I had completed college. I was scared that my memory would not return. At that point, I did not even know what I did not know. I was extremely fearful of the possibility of losing my mind and having to start over.

I was very worried that I didn't remember who they were. I do not remember how much I admired them both. Mr. Donaldson is the CEO of BUF of Michigan, a highly respected individual that I have grown to admire and adore. Mr. Evans is a dear business associate and the CEO of Evans Consulting Services, LLC, an IT support company. I met Mr. Evans on indeed, and he became like a brother to me. He was also struck by the virus and had fully recovered, yet he called to offer encouragement and some great recommendations. He encouraged me to start walking and take deep breaths. This was just what I needed at that time as I was beginning to feel extremely overwhelmed.

Sometimes, the anxiety would become so unbearable that my hands would start to shake, and I would face a severe case of tremors. I would try and play games on my phone to help with my hand-eye coordination. My memory came and went; it kept fluctuating. I was kind of hallucinating. It felt like I was two different people, and that scared me even more.

During these times, I felt like my husband was the only person I could connect with. That created a great deal of paranoia inside me. I would obsess over the fear of someone taking him away from me. I made sure he was always within my line of sight.

Whenever he disappeared from my vision, headaches, panic attacks, and tremors would overtake me. I would endure an overwhelming feeling of dread that I would scream out his name. Terry! "Are you ok," I would yell. He would calmly reply, "Yes, I'm good." I was sure I must have been getting on his nerves, but he never showed it. My walk was unsteady, and at times, I felt useless. I couldn't do anything but sit, shake, and tremble. Believe me when I say that I was going through the most terrible and confusing times that I had ever experienced.

During the day, I would cope somehow. My husband was always by my side, and that made everything a lot better. Before long, the night would come and break everything apart that I had built up during the day. I hated the nights more than anything else, especially when it was time to go to bed. One major reason was that I couldn't lay down flat on the bed. Every time I did, I would have the most severe coughing fit and would choke. It was horrible. I would also get night terrors and severe confusion. I would forget where I was and think that I was back in the hospital and, even worse, back in Mexico being trafficked. I would be so afraid that I would be scared to move.

I tried to go to sleep but couldn't. I didn't want to bother my husband as he was up all day helping me, looking after me, and supporting me, and I didn't want him to become tired and ill. One sick person in the family was enough, but I was also really frightened that he would get mad and leave me. I thought about what would happen if I had one of my coughing fits and my husband wouldn't wake up. He was my lifeline, and I was totally dependent on him.

I remember continuously asking if I was home if I was alive or dreaming. He would keep on reassuring me that I was home and that this was all real. He would keep on telling me that I wouldn't have to go back to the hospital. After three or four weeks, I started my therapy. I had physical therapy, occupational therapy, respiratory therapy, and I even saw a neurologist. I had headaches, anxiety, and so much more. It won't be wrong to say that I had almost every side effect COVID had to offer.

I have Pulmonary fibrosis - scars on my lungs. I had Encephalitis, inflammation of the brain. I have Chronic White Matter Disorder, and brain damage, and to make matters even worse, my memory was drastically being impacted. I had trouble speaking, and I've already told you about the hallucinations and the headaches. I lost my sense of smell completely, and even now, it hasn't completely returned.

I used to have an acute sense of smell. I could smell everything, and being a nurse, it was something that I relied on heavily. Not to be gross, but my sense of smell was so keen that I would smell when a woman was on her menstrual cycle. Not that I would miss that sick trick, but that's how fine-tuned my sense of smell truly was. When I battled with COVID-19 and got home, I found that I had lost it.

I lost the majority of my hair. After coming home, I couldn't bathe myself, so my husband had to clean me up. I couldn't stand in the shower. He would rub me down with lotion, comb and braid my hair, and massage my back to promote blood circulation. I started to get bedsores when I left the hospital, and his amazing care reversed the breakdown. I required a lot of care, and my husband immediately agreed to take care of me. I was grateful, but I also never felt so hopeless and useless in my entire life.

I would have nightmares about going back to the hospital. I sometimes felt like I was being kidnapped again, and if I acted well, they wouldn't torture me. These were a few of the insecurities which had attached themselves to me at home. I felt that I had to be extra nice to everyone so they wouldn't think about sending me back to the hospital. I said more thank-yous than I ever had in my life.

One day when my husband was combing my hair, I looked at the comb, and there were several long strains of hair being pulled out as he gently combed my hair. That's when I realized how fast I was shedding my hair. Then, one day, my son's girlfriend braided my hair. With French braids, I could really see how thin my hair had turned.

My hair used to be long, strong, and beautiful, and now it was literally falling off my head in handfuls. My sister Semon was truly a God-sent angel. She would call me every day and check up on me. When she called, I did not feel like I had to be strong. I could be honest with what I was going through. I cried each time she called me. Although I don't think she was aware of my daily emotional breakdowns, it was just what I needed. I hated being a burden on others. So sometimes, I was not totally honest about how I was doing. But every time I heard my sister's voice, I let go of the buildup of anxiety. Oddly enough, my sister and I were not very close. We had a few years between us, so I was always too young to really relate to her. I think we both had a desire to have a stronger connection but time got away from us. I do believe a closer relationship with my sister was a gift from God during this time. She was the first person with whom I shared pictures of my hair falling out. You could see my scalp, and I was extremely upset.

I felt like I had lost enough, and losing my hair was simply too much. During this time, she came over to see me. She had cut all her hair off. I was so shocked. She told me that she cut her hair off to support me. Although she looked amazing with short hair, I was extremely grateful for the gesture. She trimmed my hair as she saw some bald spots on my head. We decided to trim it a little but ended up trimming a lot, and I started wearing scarves. My husband told me not to wear them because, as per him, I looked like I had cancer or something. That's how bad I looked at the time.

As I became a little bit stronger, I started doing my hair on my own. I still didn't have a lot of strength, but I could rinse my hair, and as I would, gobs of it would come off into my hands. No matter what happens, for a woman, losing her hair is one of the worst things that she can ever go through. Our hair is part of our vanity. So, when I lost all my hair, I started feeling ashamed. I was utterly embarrassed by my condition and didn't want anybody to know about it. I didn't want anybody around me. But after seeing my sister rocking her new haircut, I felt a little more comfortable with the reality that my hair was gone. I let my sister cut my hair into a short little afro. She was the only one I would trust to do it. She took her time and was very supportive during this very difficult time. I know for a fact that I would not have gotten through this without her.

I also lost around 25 pounds during this time, so you can imagine what I looked like. To top it all off, my skin was extremely damaged too. My skin looked horrible. My face was splotchy, bumpy, and extremely itchy. In all honesty, I was very self-conscious and didn't want anybody to see me in this state. Don't get me wrong; I was very grateful that I was alive, and that I had survived one of the worst ordeals in my life. Honestly, I also felt a little guilty when I saw the news and learned how many people were dying and the hospitals were full. And the fact that they had to use refrigerated units outside the hospital to hold the dead. I kept asking why I was spared.

Through all this time, my husband was my rock. He was my beacon, my strength. He fed me, nursed me, and ensured that I had everything I needed and wanted. He kept telling me that I was fine and everything was going to be alright. I quickly learned that when you are not in your right mind, you need constant reassurance. I remember that I couldn't watch TV much, especially anything that had war or shooting or something like that. We ended up watching a lot of Disney, and not once did he complain about it. He just sat there beside me, held me, and watched cartoons with me all day long. He was and is still my lifeline - he and my amazing support group of friends and family. My youngest son, Terrence, always made sure that his dad had everything he needed. Anytime my husband wanted something from the store, he would go and get it. I had so much love around me that I couldn't believe it. This is what really got me through the thick and thin. People kept sending cards, flowers, texts, and more. It was amazing, and I felt truly loved and blessed.

My mom checked up on me often. She was struggling with chronic pain herself. I truly did not want to add any more stress on her. Every time she called, she would tell me to put down the phone and get some rest. I think she was also struggling with the fact that I was so close to death. My mom was so nurturing that she was always the one I turned to in both good and hard times. Lord knows I put her through quite a lot during my childhood.

I would come home from school almost every day crying because someone hurt my feelings or teased me. I did not want to burden her with my issues while she was struggling with her own. To tell you the truth, I didn't really talk too much with anyone. I was always out of breath, and my voice was extremely horse and low. It was so hoarse and painful that talking really took an effort. I just saw people on Zoom and texted them. It really helped me with my memory. When people would text me, I would look through my text history and try and remember the person I was texting. Most of the time, my memory would come back after reviewing our past conversations. But when I had limited conversations via text, my memory of them did not return. However, six months after my discharge from the hospital, I still didn't make a full recovery. I'm still facing all the complications and side effects. They finally have come up with a name for what my condition is. I think they are calling it "Long Haulers." A friend of mine, Rocky, reached out to me when I returned home. He, too, was a victim of the virus. He connected me with a Facebook COVID-19 support group.

I tried connecting with them, but most of the people in the group were people who thought they had COVID-19. They didn't know for sure or had a mild case, so I couldn't connect with them on an intimate level as they didn't have the same experience I had. I felt like nobody in the support group had any clue what I was going through. In those times, there were people who didn't go on the vent and people who never came back. I was a special case, and that made it very difficult to relate. But reading their concerns was very helpful at times, and it did take my mind off my issues.

I'm taking it one day at a time. I'm grateful for every sunrise and sunset. No more night terrors, thank God. But I know that at any time, my tremors can come back to haunt me. Although during that time, I was still struggling with headaches throughout the day. In fact, the days would turn into weeks, and it wouldn't subside. Actually, it's only been a week since I started getting some relief from my headaches.

Eight weeks with a non-stop headache is a bit much for anyone. That made it very difficult to write this book. However, as I teach in my program through my non-profit, "People become resources for your life. People may be the coach for your game. Powerful people create powerful alliances with others and allow other people to contribute to them."

My brother-in-law Dr. Mike lived in Ohio and called in a favor. He connected me with a local Neurologist who got me on her schedule to see me in record time. I had reduced my doctor's appointment wait time from two months to two weeks. I was able to receive a diagnosis of Chronic White Matter Disease. I began my treatment, but the headaches persisted. Thanks to my husband's co-worker and friend, Dr. Rob, I received some immediate relief. My husband shared my struggles with him. He recommended that I take Magnesium Glycinate 400 mg.

Through a simple conversation, my quality of life was restored. We often suffer in silence and choose to hoard our pain and sorrows in an attempt to stay private and not burden others. But the reality is that we need each other. We don't have all the answers, and sometimes we miss our blessings by remaining silent. The solutions to our most devastating problems may be closer than we think. If only we would trust God to guide us to connect with others and be transparent.

When my headaches subsided, I was able to return to work. I'm a teacher and love instilling my knowledge into young people. I started teaching from home. Although it was exhausting and I barely had the strength to get through one session, let alone three, I loved it. I'm always exhausted. I have to get lots of rest before I even think of doing anything like teaching or writing.

Still, I'm getting better day by day and am on a lot of medication. The plan is I NEED to stay healthy with no colds and no stress. I must keep my blood pressure under control to reduce further damage to my brain. I have to focus really hard to remember things. I have to keep my anxiety in check, so I'm taking antidepressants. I talk to a counselor every week. It's a lot to take in, but I'm still taking it one day at a time. Regardless of everything that I have endured and still am, I am very grateful as I know it could be much worse. I'm in a far better position than yesterday, and God willing, I will be even better tomorrow.

To support my ongoing recovery, I have changed my diet entirely, and I am on a plant-based diet. I joined this group based on my sister-in-law Robin's recommendation, called the 40-Day Turn-Up. It's a spiritual weight loss journey. Even though I had lost a substantial amount of weight while I was in the hospital, I have gained a lot during the past few months with my husband loving me through food.

With my daily routine being rest, eat, sleep, and repeat, my weight started creeping back on me with a vengeance. I'm slowly getting my weight off and trying to become healthier. I'm keeping away from things like preservatives and additives. I'm eating clean, and this program has helped me with my weight and much more. I'm sleeping much better, and my mental clarity is improving.

I'm on a slow yet correct path to getting my physical, mental, emotional, and spiritual life back, taking it one day at a time and allowing others to help. I have come so far in this journey, and as I am healing, I am enjoying living.

chapter 8

AFTERMATH

"You have dug your soul out of the dark, you have fought to be heard; do not go back to what buried you."

—*Bianca Sparacino*

"Strength In Our Scars" is a powerful statement that I read somewhere. It reminds you that you have the most strength when you are in your weakest situation. It suggests that healing can be much more than physical recovering from wounds.

I am incredibly grateful that I am recovering and physically getting better. Still, I must admit that I am emotionally tarnished and suffering. I find that my heart is broken in light of all the suffering that the world around me faces every day.

It affects me greatly and has made me fragile, to say the least. It is a word I would not have associated with myself under normal conditions. I am feeling broken, damaged, delicate, fragile, and shattered!

The old me is gone when I used to be ambitious and overly positive. I was strong and resilient and overcame every problem I faced. I was optimistic and never felt confused and disconnected. But now, I was struggling with these negative emotions. They changed me to the point where I could not identify myself.

Mind you, I still sounded the same, and I ensured that I kept everything inside hidden from my family and friends. However, I was playing an imposter. In reality, I was merely pretending that I was my former self. I was struggling with a new identity. Ironically, I wasn't sure if I wanted to be my former self anymore. I turned to prayers to find clarity. I was losing my mind and wanted to somehow correct it. I turned to God yet again and shared my problems with Him. I was scared and confused but did not want to share it with anyone else around me. I prayed, but I could not stop crying. I was hurting from the inside. It was not physical pain, but it was excruciating, nonetheless. I realized that I was mourning the death of my loved ones, especially my siblings. I became my brother's keeper, as my parents wanted me to become when I was young.

I was observing division everywhere. There was chaos wherever I looked, whether it was news, social media, or my friends and family. I was angry and anxious about everything going the wrong way. I was disappointed with what transpired in Michigan, where more than 4,000 people died in a matter of only three months. There was no leadership, and this number is even greater than 9/11.

I remember that horrible calamity quite clearly. I was at work, and the principal asked us to turn on our TV over the PA. I watched the news as the second tower was hit by a plane crashing into it. It was painful to watch people jump to their deaths. Although the entire world mourned, I remember that this atrocity brought us together as a nation.

Most of us did not know anyone who died in New York. Yet still, we strongly felt their pain and loss. We felt remorse for our collective loss. I remember that my brother told me that he was so overwhelmed by the tragedy that he had to stop driving in light of crying too much. We mourned the deaths of people killed on 9/11 and collectively surrendered our easy-flying privileges to improve security to avoid such catastrophes in the future. We allowed the rules of flying to change, and there was no major protest about it. There was no political division in America as we came up with common goals and objects, possibly for the first time in the country's history. However, I was quite nervous after 9/11. This was because I lived near an airport. However, despite this, it did not make me overanxious or more worried than an average American.

I had a discussion about this topic with my counselor Kristina. She confirmed my point that having clear leadership is vital during challenging times, and it reduces anxiety for most people. It made me uneasy how the nation did not respond to this pandemic in the same manner. It left me wondering about our nation in the current times.

Let's talk about the current situation. We have already lost hundreds of thousands of people in this pandemic. Despite this, we still fight over wearing masks in public places. I mean, seriously!

I understand that stopping work and staying indoors is tough. We all need to work to earn money and run our affairs. But weak leadership means that we are more focused on the economy rather than focusing on the loss of life. I am devastated when I see people holding signs of *"I will sacrifice the weak for our economy."* It makes you realize that today's world is different, and it has become unrecognizable.

It reminds me of Cain and Abel's story in the Bible. God asked Cain where his brother was when he had murdered Abel. Cain stated, *"I know not; am I my brother's keeper?"* This is the story that was often repeated at our house. My parents made me realize that I was a keeper. I was responsible. Once, my sister Semon had a fight after school, and my brother Andy came home without her. My mother was so angry and scolded him about it. My brother defended himself by saying, *"But she was winning the fight!"*

However, the lesson here is that YOU are responsible for your siblings. Cain asked the question to avoid responsibility, but it came back to haunt him. Cain was responsible for caring for his brother and helping him instead of being jealous. Similarly, we must care for our siblings. Most parents stress this lesson, but we find it hard to comprehend, especially when we are young.

The current state of the world with COVID-19 shows that we are moving in the wrong direction. This virus is devastating for everyone and hits all without any discrimination. Its wrath falls on everyone - the rich, the poor, white and black. It affects everyone. It has impacted food supplies, trade, financial institutions, and even closed places of worship. Just this year, the United States faced 16 natural calamities, where each has caused more than $1 billion in damage. Simultaneously, Black Lives Matter, a social movement dedicated to fighting police brutality against Black people, has also immensely impaired the social structure.

The 2020 Atlantic hurricane season has also been a historical one. It has brought 29 storms this year, beating the record of 2005. This is only the second time when English letters to name the hurricanes have been expanded.

Another hazard occurring this year was wildfires. They have destroyed many communities on the western side of the country. California has come out the worst. Fires have burned more than four million acres across the state, doubling the previous record of 2018. The largest fire of the August Complex Fire alone destroyed more than one million acres of land. It was matched by heavy rains causing high water levels in the Tittabawassee River. It destroyed dams near Midland in Michigan, forcing 10,000 residents to evacuate the region. Phoenix faced a recording of 144 days over 100 degrees Fahrenheit. Prolonged heat has resulted in many health concerns and increased weather-related deaths.

In the end, I want to get back to the statement of reminding everyone to believe in *Strength In Our Scars*. I am not alone in the healing journey. I pray that we learn from the scars of 2020 in the future and become a stronger nation through them. We must find strength in our weakest times. I am also hopeful that these injuries will enlighten our hearts and souls. They can help us come out of the dark and give us a lesson in mutual understanding. We must use these calamities to go beyond just physical healing from the economic disaster of 2020 in light of COVID-19.

I pray that we recognize and heed the warnings of the Lord. I am afraid that we will all face the worst if we don't!

chapter 9

GRATEFUL

"Everything happens for a reason. But sometimes the reason is that you're stupid and you make bad decisions."

—*Marion G. Harmon*

The Children of Israel wandered the wilderness for 40 years. I was fascinated when I read this story in the Bible but thought they were crazy. They witnessed several miracles of God and still continued to doubt His guidance and intentions. I felt how is it possible for a person to forget what God has done for them, let alone an entire group of people not understanding His purpose. I particularly wondered how these people could go astray after witnessing the parting of the Red Sea.

It also happened in such a miraculous way when all hope was lost. They must have felt doomed, but then the sea split, giving them the way across. It was an answer to prayers like none before. I am certain that they must have been full of doubt when they reached the shore and found that they were trapped. However, God had other plans for them.

I always think about this story when I am facing hardship. I turn to this story when I seemingly reach a dead-end situation. I contemplate why it took them forty years to find comfort. Why did they not believe in God, knowing that He would save them from any situation? He had repeatedly showered on them His mercy and bounty.

I read this story several times, but all of a sudden, it spoke to me intimately. I understood that when they were wandering around, they must have lost faith. They became lost, and their current reality occupied them. They believed that everything was bleak and could do nothing to get out of it. However, it made them fully dependent on God's favor as they exhausted all other options. I found that I was no different. I was as stuck as they were. I was also wandering in my desert, not realizing that God's bounty is enough for me, just as it was enough for the Children of Israel.

I had a plethora of problems. Some of my struggles were linked to family chaos, work problems, parenting issues, reading disability, and terrible health. Yes, it all equates to wandering around in life without purpose. I was going from one tragedy to another, never thinking about how the process was changing me for the better, like a lump of coal going through extreme pressure and heat for it to crystallize and become a beautiful diamond. As I look back now, I can truly see my crystallization process. God orchestrated the chain of events to develop me into the person that He wanted me to become.

While I was going through this period of enlightenment, I had this great urge to clean and declutter my house. To be quite honest, when I came home from the hospital, I looked at how cluttered my closet was and thought how happy I was that I survived. I would have been mortified if anyone had seen my disgustingly messy closet. I started watching this program called, Tidying Up with Marie Kondo. She has a unique way of cleaning. She encourages you to start by taking all your clothing and putting them in one area. Yes, all your clothing. Through her process, you are to go through each item and get rid of everything you do not have a connection with.

Needless to say, I have a lot of stuff. I have two walk-in closets, two dressers, and three large under-bed bends. There was a mountain of clothes on my bed and falling on the floor and everywhere. I was in shock as I looked at all this shit. Sorry for the profanity, but that is the best way for me to describe what I was looking at. I saw years and years of stuff that I had been stockpiling and hiding in my closets. Wow, it was overwhelming and painful at times. But I was obedient and patiently went through the process.

One by one, I measured my emotions toward each piece of clothing. As I collected bag after bag of discarded pieces, I literally felt the stress leave me. By the end of the day, everything was sorted, and I felt so free. I shared this experience with my sons and compared this unique decluttering experience with my choice to declutter myself. I was given an amazing gift - the gift of life. I wanted to make sure that I was very intentional about what stayed a part of my new way of being and what had to go.

I, too, was hiding a lot of garbage in my spirit. Garbage that was dictating my views, attitudes, and disposition. I also taught this process. However, let me honestly say that teaching and living are entirely two different things. I am the author of my life, and I get to say what I want and don't want in my life. When my desires aligned with what God wanted for me, it felt just like plowing through the pile of mess on my bed. I felt free.

I still believe that I am still changing and improving, and I have a long way to go. I want to be better still and don't wish to be the person I was before this ordeal. I want to stay away from my old thoughts and grab the new opportunities of life unfolding in front of me. I must defeat the lack of balance in my life and get out of developing a victim mentality. I must get ahead of fear and feel fragile by believing in God and His ability to mold me into a better and more capable person.

These old thoughts have no room in my new world. Being disconnected from God shook my entire core and forced me to get back to Him. If I want to reach my promised land, I must submit to God's will and follow His path. I yearn to be in God's will and become His instrument.

I read on a poster, "When I say, I feel so empty, God says, I created you with a longing in your heart that only I can feel." It describes the message of Psalm 90:14. It says, "Satisfy us early with thy mercy; that we may rejoice and be glad all our days."

I yearn for the peace promised by God, and I yearn to reach the promised land, even if it is only in my mind.

chapter 10

REBIRTH

"And as she fell apart, her shattered pieces began to bloom - blossoming until she became herself exactly as she was meant to be."

—Becca Lee

Although my COVID recovery journey has been extremely tough, I am incredibly thankful. The lessons I have learned through my healing process have helped me in many ways. I have a different perspective on life, proving that you can teach old dogs new tricks. It is not impossible to change and evolve after 50. The problem is most of us do not realize that we need transformation.

Sometimes, we are oblivious to our flaws and the need for change. When or if we recognize that we need to make some changes in our lives, we do not know where to start. We only know that we are unhappy, unfulfilled, and unsatisfied with who we are or our lives in general. This feeling of unfulfillment leaves us with a vast void. We often focus on filling the gap with sinless compromises; as a medical professional, I use the expression, "We put a Band-Aid over a gunshot wound," which is useless. Nevertheless, we attempt to fix our brokenness with temporary fixes that are not sustainable or realistic.

We gravitate to an unhealthy relationship. We may go on a shopping spree, eat until we almost explode, push people out of our lives, or even start using drugs, drinking, or even self-harm. None of which are solutions. They are just Band-Aids, temporary fixes. Many of us may even hide our unhappiness from our loved ones and attempt to win an Emmy for the best actor. We are smiling while hiding the fact that we are miserable. Sometimes the Lord uses this time in our lives to draw us nearer to Him. When you are brought to your knees and see no way out, you find yourself calling out His name. Lord, help me! One scripture that I hold on to during times of hopelessness is Matthew 11:28 -30, "Come to me, all you who are weary and burdened, and I will give you rest. Take my yoke upon you and learn from me, for I am gentle and humble in heart, and you will find rest for your souls. For my yoke is easy, and my burden is light."

I often meditate on God's word during hard times. During my medical challenges, I found myself reciting scripture that I had hidden in my heart over the years. It amazes me how relevant God's word is and how it provides such comfort. I am still suffering from difficulty breathing at times, struggling with thinking and concentration (sometimes referred to as "brain fog"), a sore throat, muscle pain, headaches, and depression.

Although physically, I have been scarred by COVID's wrath, ironically, I am more motivated, positive, and focused than ever. I have always been extremely self-motivated and driven, but I lacked balance. One would think it is impossible to suffer from depression while being motivated and having a balanced life. But that is my reality. Statistically, the symptoms of depression include a lack of interest in things and not feeling motivated. But I am experiencing just the opposite.

I believe that the source of my motivation is different than most. I am more concerned about what God wants for me vs. what I want for me. I am more focused on seeking His will and reflecting on His word (the Bible) to gain wisdom while evaluating and measuring my imperfections. My goal is not to be sinless but to sin less and become more like Christ.

I remember sitting in my recliner in my room in the middle of the night. My husband was sound asleep. I was too afraid to move because I was experiencing night terrors. It was difficult for me to breathe. I was coughing, and hallucinating, and I thought I was dying. I started to shiver, and I could hear my teeth chatter. I remember crying while trying to be quiet. I did not want anyone to find me and torture me. I was not in a good place.

After suffering for what felt like hours, I remember crying out to the Lord and asking him to take away my fear. I was desperate. I did not ask Him to take away the coughing, insomnia, or even breathing difficulty. I just wanted to be free of fear. "Lord, please help me," I cried. "Please take away my fear." I did not want to ask for too much. I felt like He would be mad at me. I don't think I have ever been so desperate. I did not plead my case or even repeat my prayer. I prayed, and then I sat in my chair and waited for Him to deliver me.

I stayed with expectation as if I was sure that he would come through for me, and He did. He delivered me, and I felt that familiar presence I had felt in the hospital and an overwhelming sense of peace. As I think about it, I can't help but cry. How could I ever go back to "normal," back to the old me, after feeling God's presence? I felt complete, protected, and safe; it's hard to explain it. It was everything good. Thank you, Lord.

The next morning, I received a call from a former student Willie. He is a paramedic and a herbalist. He was calling to check on me. He specifically asked me about my coughing and sleeping. I thought it was random, but I felt comfortable sharing what I was experiencing. He recommended marshmallow and coltsfoot herbs tea to help with breathing. He also made me a mixture of different herbs and bee pollen. Pollen contains many vitamins, minerals, and antioxidants, making it incredibly healthy. Studies have linked bee pollen and its compounds to health benefits such as decreased **inflammation** and improved immunity. Willie was God-sent, and his concoction worked. God even answered my unasked prayers.

"Do not be anxious about anything, but in every situation, by prayer and petition, with thanksgiving, present your requests to God. And the peace of God, which transcends all understanding, will guard your hearts and your minds in Christ Jesus." Philippians 4:6-7

The last few months have been a 'real game-changer' for me, and I love every moment of my new me. My life has more balance and purpose. I am selfish with my time and laser-focused and do not sweat the small stuff. I am motivated for self-improvement, prioritize time for my daily devotion and prayer, and organize my surroundings by decluttering my house. Although my routine has changed by working from home, I take more care of myself by taking naps during the day when needed, watching my diet, and exercising. I am much happier with my improved mental state. I continue to meet with my therapist and do the work. Although my flesh still craves my guilty pleasures, I am so thankful that I have become more confident, happier, and relaxed than ever before.

I don't know what's next for me, but the Lord surely knows. I am patiently waiting on His direction and guidance. I think that I have put my hand in that flame way too many times, not knowing that trying to go ahead of the Lord will get me burnt. Therefore, I am working on trusting His word, Isaiah 40:31, "But they who wait for the LORD shall renew their strength; they shall mount up with wings like eagles; they shall run and not be weary; they shall walk and not faint." I guess I never really understood what it meant to wait on the Lord and was oblivious to the concept's true meaning. Although I have been given those instructions quite often, I still approached life like a child getting ready to jump into swinging ropes, like Double Dutch, impatiently rocking back and forth. I was waiting for that perfect moment to jump in without being swapped by a rope or being tangled up. Yes, that was me, making a decision, following through with it, and then praying that God would bless my mess.

Looking back at all my poor choices and thinking about how I was confused about why things turned out the way they did, I was not waiting on the Lord. I was actually seeking my wisdom, trusting myself, and throwing a prayer or two at the end for good measure. I think that previously I wasn't trusting God the way I trust him now. One of the most amazing gifts that my rebirth has given me is 'infinite faith' and trust in God's plans for me. Before that, I was always slick. I spoke the "Christianese," as my friend Dr. Fleda would say. I knew how to talk 'the talk,' but I did not always walk the walk. There were many times when I used to share my religious point of view with people but had a hard time following them myself. Lord, forgive me!

I learned that waiting on the Lord requires great effort at first but gradually takes you to a place of total peace and tranquility. I have learned that in order to wait on the Lord, you must Trust, Seek Him, and Pray.

Possessing the ability to trust someone is very difficult for most people truly. I know that I have made a commitment on several occasions to trust the Lord and give Him all my care, only to find myself taking it back from Him. While being in such a desperate situation, with no family, friends, or hope, I did not feel like I had a choice. So I let go and left everything in His hands.

The moment you start thinking about holding God's hand, all your worries and sorrows become bearable. That was one of the best moments of my life, believe me. You literally feel as if somebody is offering you a shoulder and trying to comfort you. You hear the Lord whisper in your ear, *"You have handled everything enough on your own, now give all your worries and fears to me."* I don't think that I'll ever be able to put that beautiful feeling into words. The way it calms your soul and finally brings it to peace after a long time of being lost.

My new perspective on life has confirmed my purpose, and finally, I have a clearer path and direction for my future. I am ready to accept whatever comes my way now. I know that God is watching me and will always protect me from every hardship and sorrow, as long as I have faith in Him.

Sometimes, I wonder what if that whole incident had not taken place, and I had not experienced COVID and gone through my recovery process? I wonder how people get through this type of experience without the Lord. Although my journey is not over, I now understand why God chose me for all this. I feel so grateful that I am finally becoming the person that I am meant to be. I would often question my strong desire to work with and help youth and young adults, specifically during times of business stagnation for my non-profit. I had doubts about my program and what I was teaching through the Nurturing Wellness Group Foundation. I questioned whether I was truly making the type of impact that I claimed. My journey definitely allowed me to test the concepts that I teach. I had often poured these concepts into my students, children, and my family. I was able to use them on a very intimate level for myself. Particularly the lesson on the importance of cultivating positive relationships.

In my opinion, as long as we remain physically and emotionally strong, we do not realize the true value of the relationships around us. It's when only we are faced with hardships; that we realize how much support we have, and that God has blessed us with so much love around us. I remember that there were times in my life when I would question my existence. I used to ask myself, *'Why am I even alive?'* I have felt, as I am sure, we have all felt as if you are a burden on your family and others. But now, during these times of uncertainty, God is using it to draw us closer to others and Himself. I believe that our relationships are tested during times of hardship. In your good times, everybody can stay with you and love you, but only a few loyal people stay with you in your tough times too. I feel so blessed to have a supportive social circle of friends and family who never left me alone, even for a second. My best friend Tykee has gone above and beyond to help me. She cooked, cleaned, and just sat with me during my most difficult times. My business partner Carla is truly a blessing. Not only is she my partner, but she is also my friend. We take turns lifting each other up as we hold each other accountable while supporting youth. Just like little gifts from God. A call from Kim (my classmate from nursing school) or a text from Afreida (my best friend after high school), a contact from family members I had not seen in years, calling just to say, "How are you doing," just when I needed it. Right on time.

While being surrounded by all this love, I could not help but feel sad for people who do not have the same support as I do. People tend to block people from their life for many reasons, pride, shame, unforgiveness, you name it. I especially see this with our youth. I have a special space in my heart for young people. It makes me sad to see how some of our youths are being targeted for horrible things. They become lost and hopeless in part due to their lack of healthy relationships. This is evident by the rate of Suicide for this age group. Suicide is the second leading cause of death for young people ages 15-24. That breaks my heart.

We are seeing a lot of hate groups and trafficking activity targeting our youth and young adults. A lot of efforts are being made for awareness, but little has been done to support prevention. My programs provide a platform that will support personal growth and prevent high-risk behaviors that lead to vulnerability in introducing these types of influences. Our youth are also ill-equipped with adequate soft skills to provide future industries with quality, dependable, and committed employees. This lack of preparation is drastically impacting our workforce. Our program supports soft development skills by providing our participants with project-based programming to support their development and growth.

I truly believe that prevention starts with equipping our young people with the skills and tools needed to build their confidence and motivation for their future lives.

In my opinion, some of the hardships that I went through were sent my way to train me. It was to prepare me for my assignment to pursue my passion. Although my journey has blessed me with lots of hope, faith, and love, I think the best gift it has given me is 'trust.' My trust in God is growing more and more with every passing day, and I feel much calmer and more relaxed now. According to my beliefs, trust is to believe in the reliability, truth, or strength of something. It is to have confidence and expectation.

I believe that trust in people is built over time. It starts when you are young. I remember when my youngest son was learning how to swim. He would jump in the pool only after getting my husband's attention to catch him. He knew the water was dangerous, but he trusted his father to catch him.

My son's trust in my husband has grown through the years, which time has only cemented, making it firmer. But before the trust, he had faith in his father, the size of a muster seed that eventually blossomed into unwavering trust. Now, this is what always confused me. It was clear that trust was birth by faith. So, what birthed faith? Faith comes through hearing the Word of God, through the convicting and drawing work of the Holy Spirit. It comes through responding to the revelation that one has already received from God. We cannot trust someone we don't know, and that is the secret of learning to trust God. If my son did not know his father, he would not have ever jumped in the water. When someone says, "Trust me," we have one of two reactions. Either we can say, "Yes, I'll trust you," or we can say, "Why should I?" In God's case, trusting Him follows when we understand why we should. So, before we can trust God, we must first know Him. Jesus came to earth, died on the cross, and was raised to life to rescue you from sin. Your Salvation is God's gift to you. It is not earned by anything you do. So, before you can even attempt to wait on the Lord, you must be saved.

> Hear the gospel of Christ (Rom 10:11-17)
>
> Have faith (belief) in Christ (Rom 1:16-17, 8:34)
>
> Repent of sin (Rom 2:4-5, 6:1-2)
>
> Confess faith in Christ (Rom 10:8-10)
>
> Be baptized into Christ (Rom 6:3-4, 8:1)
>
> Continue in his way (Rom 12:1-2, 12:11-12)

I believe that Salvation from sin was the purpose of Jesus' life, death, and resurrection. Therefore, it plays an important part in one's spiritual journey. I would like to share some steps to Salvation by Grace with you that will help you with your journey with the Lord.

I have learned that in order to wait on the Lord, you must have Trust; Seek Him; and Pray. My faith in the Lord is the substance of things hoped for, the evidence of things not seen (Hebrews 11:1). Waiting on the Lord involves the confident expectation of a positive result, even if the path of deliverance comes through COVID-19. As I missioned prior to becoming sick, I was struggling for a few years with forgiveness, anger, resentment, and a humongous load of other emotional burdens.

I was a child of God, so I had faith, and I trusted that He would deliver me. Because I did not feel His presence due to my disobedience, I began to seek Him. I did not actually realize what I was doing. I did not sense His presence and was desperate for it. Both the Old and New Testaments say that Seeking God is a "setting of the mind and heart" on God. It is the conscious fixing or focusing on our mind's attention and our heart's affection for Him. "Now set your mind and heart to seek the Lord your God" (1 Chronicle 22:19). I was having a hard time praying during this time, and going to church was very difficult. I listened to biblical messages and sought wisdom through his word. I began to pray for wisdom and thank Him for everything. I thanked Him for very small things at first, like the sun shining or the rain pouring down. Then, I started to thank Him for my safety in travel, my health, and the health of my family. Then my prayer life became stronger and stronger as the days passed. Although I still could not feel His presence, my faith was restored.

I know that I would not have survived this ordeal without my connection to God and all the concepts that I teach through my program, which is grounded in biblical principles. I feel so strongly now about my calling that a percentage of this book's profits will be donated to support youth who participate in my program. So, thank you for helping me change lifes through your purchase of this book. It gives me immense pleasure to think about how many others will benefit from my spiritual journey.

The Lord most definitely used my season of hardship to draw me closer to himself. I can't believe how much I have grown. I've grown enough to know that I have a lot of growing to do. Looking back over my life, I am extremely thankful for every tear, heartache, and struggle. Without them, I wouldn't have known the power of God's grace. It is grounded in a profound level of respect and admiration that I have discovered that leads me to say, *"I am truly Grateful for the Journey."*

chapter 11

CONCLUSION

This book uses stories from my life to explain how we cannot control trials, but we can surely choose how we deal with them. It varies from person to person whether we use our pain as an opportunity to grow further or whether we just live through it without embracing the lesson.

We need to understand that nobody in this whole world is living a 'problem-free' life. We all have problems and hurdles that are a part of our life journey. I believe that challenges and obstacles are important parts of our lives, as they help us become stronger.

Life is hard sometimes, and we are powerless when it comes to misfortune. Misfortune is unpredictable, may be extremely stressful, and can cause a great deal of pressure. However, pressure is what turns a lump of coal into a diamond. I believe that God uses this same process to develop our character, so we are prepared to carry out our purpose.

A couple of days ago, I came across a wonderful quote, *"What doesn't kill you makes you stronger."* It hit me really hard. I strongly believe that my painful recovery process, especially the ventilator, has given me so much strength that now I don't sweat the small stuff. I am ready for whatever challenges life throws at me now because I have already been through so much. I remember that I was extremely depressed and hopeless during my hospital stay. I used to ask God again and again, *"Lord, why me? What have I done to be in this place?"* I pleaded with Him to spare me because I wanted to live for my children, family, and unfinished business.

Looking back at those times now, the only emotion that comes to mind is gratitude. I am extremely thankful to be where I am now. I know that I am still recovering, and it will still take me some time to fully recover, but I am so glad that God listened to our prayers. He blessed me with a new and much better perspective on life.

Dark times come and go, but what remains forever is the love and support of the people around you. I can't thank the Lord enough for blessing me with such wonderful friends and family who were always there to support me, especially my mother, husband, children, sisters, and brothers. I don't remember even a single day when they left me alone to get depressed. They did not let me overthink at all and made sure that I was okay.

I believe that relationships are tested during hard times because everybody stays by your side when you are in full power. I am so grateful that God has blessed me with the most loving and supportive husband ever. He has always been there for me in all good and bad times. I don't think that I would ever be able to describe my love for him in words. Thankfully, our bond is getting stronger with every passing minute. This whole journey has truly tested his love, in which he always exceeded my expectations.

I believe that your mindset plays an extremely important part in shaping your life because whatever you think becomes your reality. We need to train our minds to believe in positivity so that we live a happier and more peaceful life. I keep telling my children and students that life is just as complicated or peaceful as we think. It totally depends on us how well we get along with the new life changes or struggles. We can either accept those changes happily, grow through them, or just remain unhappy and let the changes consume us.

We need to understand that pain is an inevitable part of our lives, and nobody is free from it. So why not accept it wholeheartedly and consider it as a source of growth. We need to develop the ability to cope with the inevitable consequences of hardship. Unfortunately, we do not possess the skills to do so, and it may take a lifetime before we can truly escape the wrath of its impact.

This fact has motivated my life's work of pouring into young people by helping them discover a new way of living by creating a new way of thinking. I help them reframe their current reality so they can perceive a new possibility for their life. This new perspective is provided by the Nurturing Wellness Group Foundation's programs, "Life Support for Students, and Young Adult Support System." The Nurturing Wellness Group Foundation helps young people overcome barriers that prevent or delay school and life success by providing them access to a holistic support system.

Recently, Glennon Doyle Melton said in her discussion with Oprah, *"Pain is a traveling professor and it goes and knocks on everyone's door. The smartest people I know are the people who say, come in and don't leave until you have taught me what I need to know."* I think that it is absolutely true. Wise people are always looking for more options to grow, and pain is the most powerful source of growth. So, they welcome it wholeheartedly, learn through it, and then say goodbye to it after using it fully for their advantage.

It is always our hurt that cracks us open and lets the light come inside us. Our pain shows us the right direction and tells us how we can live a more fulfilling life. I have never seen anyone in this whole world who behaves the same way after going through a painful experience or hardship. We all have our ways to learn. Pain makes us go through some life-changing psychological shifts in our thinking and attitude, giving us the energy to become stronger and sharper than before.

Today, I feel so happy to look back at all those times when I was helpless. I feel that God sent all that pain my way just to make me realize that He is in control. My experience has taught me that life is too short to be spent on things that we aren't passionate about, and it is only wise to reflect on our God-given gifts. We should live our lives to the fullest and always give all our love and support to our loved ones because we never know when our time on this earth will be up. There should be no regrets in our hearts while leaving this world.

I do realize that not everybody is as blessed as me to receive a 'new' life. And I truly value this fact. Now I want to live my life better and share all my life experiences with other people so that they benefit from my lessons. I have become humbler and more affectionate toward people because I know that all humans are equal. None of us has power over our fortunes. I have tried my best to teach my children that 'respect' and 'love' are extremely important. I also stress that we can never have too much kindness in the world. No matter what you are going through in life, always remember to be kind. Everybody has their battles that we know nothing about. Sometimes as Christians, we are the only light they see. We must represent God's love through our kindness. You never know the impact you may have on others just by simply being kind. Being kind can show up as the very thing that is needed to give someone hope. Sometimes, all you need is a little hope.

I still remember the time when I was sitting on the toilet, and the nurse aide embraced me and raked my hair with her fingers. I wanted to scream but couldn't. I had no idea if I would ever get a chance to get back home or not. I used to think about all those times when I was happy and healthy with my family. It felt as if somebody had stabbed me in my heart with a knife and twisted it. I was emotionally exhausted and had lost all hope. But her act of kindness was all I needed to pull me out of the depths of my defeat. She restored my hope.

I remember how everybody was clapping for me when I came out of the hospital after a 29-day-long battle with COVID-19. During that time, surviving the ventilator was no less than a miracle for me. It has been almost a year, but sometimes I still wonder how I made it. But I do know that God answers prayers and has blessed me exceedingly and abundantly more than I could have ever imagined. God used my healing journey from COVID-19 to reveal my joy, my Tragedy to tell my Truth, and my Fear to expose my Freedom. With this book, I want to inspire my readers to live life on purpose and be more productive with the time they have been given. I want you all to remember that it's only our hard times that make us realize our real worth. No matter what you are going through in life, just have faith in God's plans for you.

Finally, I want to thank you all for purchasing this book and giving me a chance to convey my message to the world. Your support will help me reach our youth as I walk out the calling on my life. I hope that you have found value in sharing my journey with me. Each word of this book has been written prayerfully with an immense amount of love and warmth to motivate you to live a better life and be the best version of yourself. It is my prayer that God heals all your pain and allows you to find peace in your journey as you discover your true purpose.

ACKNOWLEDGMENTS

To my husband,

Terry, I love you with all my heart. I am so very blessed to have you. You're my soul mate and my best friend (see, I said it). Thank you for always having my back and never being afraid to let me shine. I love you.

To Travis and Terrance,

I am so proud to be your mom. You are my heart and truly a gift from God. Thank you for being strong and supporting dad during this difficult time. I love you!

To my family,

Winston, for your strength and wisdom.
Semon, for your unwavering love, support, and friendship.
Robin, for your prayers, guidance, support, and wisdom.
Afreida, for your love, friendship, and consistency.
Shanta, for providing crucial care as an RN on the COVID-19 unit during the pandemic while lifting patients up in prayer, maintaining your house, and ministering to my family during this time. Words cannot express how grateful I am for you and your selfless contribution. You are amazing.

To all my brothers, in-laws, cousins, and family members who reached out to my family and me while holding us up in prayer. Please know that you are appreciated.

To my friends,

Tykee M., Carla S., Thalia S., Lisa W., Willie B., Kim H., Lewis Family, Willie B., Robin W. NWGF Board Members, Friends, and P-CEP Administration. Thank you for your prayers, calls, cards, understanding, and unbelievable tokens of love and support to myself and my family during our difficult time.

To my Church family,

Pastor Larry Johnson, REAL Woman ministry, and my church family. Thank you for exemplifying God's word, "So then, as we have the opportunity, let us do good to everyone, and especially to those who are of the household of faith." Galatians 6:10. Thank you!

Thank you, Lord: "Fear thee not, for I am with thee, be not dismayed for I am your God; I will strengthen thee, yea, I will help thee, I will uphold thee with the right hand of my righteousness. (Isa. 41:10)"

"Thank you, Lord, for Grace and Mercy." A. Terry Brinston.

www.ingramcontent.com/pod-product-compliance
Lightning Source LLC
Chambersburg PA
CBHW051220120626
46547CB00013B/1438